Praise for Tic

It goes without saying that teachers are incr
this activity, it's all too easy for even the mos
vital information, misplace crucial resources a... ...., ..., ...
promised they will remember. Harry Fletcher-Wood's timely and useful book
draws on examples from the safety-critical industries like healthcare and aviation
to recommend one simple, straightforward and easy-to-implement addition to
ensure the best laid plans of overworked teachers do not go awry.

Interesting, practical and accessible, this little book and its one big idea could
transform the way you work. Highly recommended.

**David Didau, author of *What If Everything
You Knew About Education Was Wrong?***

Harry has created a book for those of us who lose worksheets, misplace pens
and don't have a calm, organised person upstairs. But instead of making teachers
feel bad for disorganisation he offers a solution: a simple, effective, thought-
provoking aid for getting through each and every situation the classroom (and
its chaos) has on offer. When I was in the classroom, I constantly wondered what
the best way to organise myself was. This book does the hard-work thinking for
you, but still encourages you to think some more!

Laura McInerney, editor, *Schools Week*

I am admittedly a fan of checklists and I am now also a fan of *Ticked Off*. In
a world stuffed full of busyness, a checklist can help bring clarity and calm.
Harry Fletcher-Wood takes a systematic approach to creating usable checklists
for pretty much every aspect of school life. This book is a pleasure to read and
helped me think more clearly about the complexity of our daily work as teachers.

Is Harry's book on checklists immensely valuable and worth your precious
time? Tick! Is it an easy read that proves practical and useful? Tick! Should busy
teachers invest in this book? Tick!

**Alex Quigley, teacher, Huntington School,
author of *Teach Now! English***

Harry's book acts as an empathetic guide to support efficiency, balancing the
complexities of education as a whole and the role of being a teacher. This is not
necessarily a how-to style book; it shares Harry's reflections on what works for
him and the understandings he has, offering measured and balanced reflections
for improving as students, teachers, leaders; and within teaching itself. In sharing
his perceptions of his practice, and how he has subsequently developed, the
reader cannot help but consider their own practice and embark upon a journey
in which their own styles are audited.

I love that this book is not written by a stereotypically organised person. For the rest of us who struggle at this, Harry isn't condescending or judgemental and has an approachable, comfortable tone; it's as if you're sat in the staffroom chatting with him!

Kieran Dhunna Halliwell (Ezzy_Moon), researcher and consultant

Ticked Off takes its approach from Atul Gawande's *The Checklist Manifesto*, which demonstrates how checklists help to improve standards and avoid errors. Following examples from the fields of science and medicine, Harry Fletcher-Wood shows how aspects of teaching and organisation can be managed more easily by using checklists.

Irrespective of the ultimate complexity of the task on hand, a checklist simplifies the task by breaking it down into manageable entities. The real beauty of this book is that the checklists are easy to use and can be adapted for all aspects of teaching and working within education, from nursery and primary school levels through to higher education. All education practitioners will find practical resources to improve their own practice, to lead and train others, to introduce and implement sustainable changes, to deal with difficult conversations, to lead meetings effectively, to gauge student voice and feedback and to involve students by making them responsible for their own learning.

Ticked Off is a great book, offering an interesting and practical approach to time management. Having read this book I am now implementing checklists in my own work. If you only have time to read one education book this year, make sure it is this one because this is a fantastic resource.

**Nicole Brown, lecturer in education and
secondary teacher education programme leader**

Anyone familiar with Harry's writing will know very well how thorough, thoughtful and subtly profound he is. He takes the ordinary and makes us look at it sideways, upside-down and inside-out. Harry challenges us to revisit the everyday to ensure that our bread and butter is the best it can be. Harry's admiration for Atul Gawande has led him to create a book about teaching and learning, and what a treasure trove it is. In *Ticked Off*, Harry approaches the oft ignored parts of our day with precision and vigour to try to help us be incrementally better through effective planning and use of the simple checklist: how can students best know if they're ready for exams, or if their essays are excellent? How might teachers help their students master vocabulary, or ensure that that poor lesson never repeats itself? What about being ready for trips, observations and giving feedback?

This is a book for everyone: student, teacher, middle leader and leader. But it's also personable, honest, thorough and important. It's Harry Fletcher-Wood all over, and every school needs a copy.

Toby French (@MrHistoire), history teacher

Practical ✓
Useful ✓
Transformational ✓

Ticked off

CHECKLISTS for
Teachers ✓
Students ✓
School leaders ✓

Harry Fletcher-Wood

Crown House Publishing Limited
www.crownhouse.co.uk

First published by

Crown House Publishing
Crown Buildings,
Bancyfelin,
Carmarthen,
Wales, SA33 5ND, UK
www.crownhouse.co.uk

and

Crown House Publishing Company LLC
6 Trowbridge Drive, Suite 5, Bethel, CT 06801, USA
www.crownhousepublishing.com

First published 2016. Reprinted 2016.

British Library Cataloguing-in-Publication Data

A catalogue entry for this book is available from the British Library.

Print ISBN: 978-1-78583-010-5
Mobi ISBN: 978-1-78583-063-1
ePub ISBN: 978-1-78583-064-8
ePDF ISBN: 978-1-78583-065-5

LCCN 2015953328

Printed and bound in the UK by
Gomer Press, Llandysul, Ceredigion

For my parents.

Foreword by Sir Tim Brighouse

Like the author, I am not a natural fan of checklists.

The roots of my dislike can probably be traced to having an excellent memory when I was young and being a bit over-pleased with myself for that good fortune, which for a long time I assumed was connected with our view at that time about what it was to be intelligent. My attitude is best illustrated by anecdote. As a very young deputy at Chepstow Community College in the mid-1960s I worked with a head towards the end of his career whose working practice included summoning me each morning for a briefing. I recall thinking him rather pathetic for having a 'list' in his hand as he ran through what needed to be done that day and I remember his puzzlement that I didn't take any notes of the many tasks he required of me. I had no difficulty in recall. Now of course, I not only need lists but often find I can't remember where I have put them!

But my prejudice against lists had two further aspects. First, I thought checklists the enemy of creativity, especially in teaching, which I saw as more of an art than a science, and therefore 'lists' were to be avoided at all costs. Second, when I later deployed weekly 'to do' lists drawn up on a Sunday evening for the following week, I became depressed at my inability to tick any of them off as the crises of the days that followed displaced them and the urgent overtook the important. I even considered the temptation recounted to me by a Scottish educator of adding things on a Friday that had already been done simply to gain the pleasure of ticking them off.

So like Harry Fletcher-Wood, I approached Atul Gawande's *The Checklist Manifesto* with some scepticism. But like all good books it caused me to think. Of course I had long realised that good management and administration is about 'doing things right' to complement the strategic imperative of doing the 'right things'. For schools, this was best expressed by the Victorian Head of Uppingham who once said, 'I take my stand on detail'. So I accepted, in the administration and management of schools, checklists had their place. Of course this book will show you how the checklist has an essential role in good and effective lessons and learning. Perhaps the primary practitioner has always known that: certainly the widespread practice of giving pupils regular tasks – the classroom monitor syndrome – relies on the checklist approach. This book takes our thinking so much further with an abundance of practical examples.

As schools wrestle with the conundrum of what are the 'non-negotiables' in their teaching and learning policy and practice, and as they seek to strike a balance between 'singing from the same song sheet', yet not doing so to the extent that they hem the individual teacher in with so many 'must dos' that they stifle creativity, they'll find this book more than useful – in practice an invaluable aid to discussion in whole school, departmental and phase meetings.

In a primary classroom the other day, I had a glimpse of practice which I thought reflected the surgical practice outlined in *The Checklist Manifesto* where Gawande explains how consultants were initially resistant to the checklist approach and were only won over by the nurse taking the role of running through the checklist in the operating theatre since for the consultant to do so was an affront to dignity. In the classroom I caught sight of two year 6 pupils at the start of the session who were running through the requirements of the teacher's lesson plan as she smilingly looked on, nodding as it came to issues affecting her; the rest of the class also checked as it came to issues that would involve them playing their part in what was to unfold.

So I commend this book as a stimulus to improving practice in schools and classrooms across the country. It will lead to better learning for pupils and, as I saw the other day, perhaps their involvement in the checklist process.

Sir Tim Brighouse, former London Schools Commissioner and Chief Education Officer for Birmingham and Oxfordshire

Acknowledgements

Louisa King helped inspire me to begin work on the book; Bodil Isaksen, Tim Brighouse and David Didau offered insightful comments on early drafts and Doug Lemov provided much needed encouragement at a critical stage. Andy Day, David Didau and @ImSporticus generously allowed me to use their work. Inasmuch as the checklists contain good ideas, they reflect the actions and ideas of everyone I've ever worked alongside, been trained by or been fortunate enough to see teach – thank you.

Contents

iii. Checklists for teachers 77

iv. Checklists for leaders 101

Introduction

Why checklists?

Two years ago, I would have dismissed the thought of writing a book promoting checklists to fellow teachers: I saw the impersonal routine they implied as stifling. In any case, my own organisation was too haphazard to venture advice to anyone else. Both my views and my efficiency have since changed: this book seeks to share the process and the result.

As teachers, many things prevent us from achieving all that we would like, but most come down to a single cause: while students' needs are infinite, our time and resources are not. Were we to itemise everything we would like to do for every student in all our classes for a single day – marking books, planning lessons, having supportive individual conversations and so on – and then add up the time these tasks demand, I suspect we would reach a total in excess of a reasonable week's work. Additional external and unsought factors add to this pressure – moving classrooms, evidencing our work for Ofsted, specification changes – but they are simply a bitter icing; the cake is unpalatable because students' needs are so extensive. Our time will never suffice for all we hope to do, so it pays to be as efficient as possible.

Some teachers seem intimidatingly organised in all they do. Neat stacks of paper, appropriately labelled and organised, set out everything their students may need each day; by the afternoon, worksheets have been completed diligently, resources filed carefully, work marked constructively and all is ready for tomorrow. This book is not designed for such paragons.

This book is for everyone else. We manage most of the time, with occasional heart-stopping moments as we realise, or fear, that we've committed a gigantic oversight. If you've ever started a lesson and realised you haven't printed enough copies of an essential worksheet, this book is for you. If you've struggled with the number of students who need help completing a simple task which you're sure you've explained clearly, this book is for you. If you've ever crawled to colleagues or managers to apologise that the data, seating plans or replies they expected have slipped your mind, this book is for you.

We're not bad people or bad teachers. We manage our mistakes. We reprint lesson resources and send students to collect the worksheets, anxiously filling the intervening time. We run around the classroom trying to help every student, not quite managing, and ending with a dull sense that the lesson didn't quite work out – a sense quickly over-whelmed by the rush of the next class's arrival. We make our apologies to colleagues and struggle on to our next lapse. We chalk up our mistakes and omissions as an inevitable part of the everyday struggle that is being a teacher, and assume that it's meant to be this way.

This book offers something different. Checklists can free us to devote our time, energy and attention to focusing on the tasks that matter most.

who uses checklists?

This book takes its inspiration from Atul Gawande's fascinating book, *The Checklist Manifesto*.* Gawande describes a process of research, seeking to understand how checklists are used in flying and construction, and his subsequent attempts to build on these insights by developing equiva-lents in his own field, surgery.

Gawande highlights the importance of checklists to pilots. He gives examples of crashes in which, by fixating on individual problems – like restarting an engine – pilots have overlooked basic procedures – like mon-itoring the aeroplane's height. Gawande shows how the airline industry prevents such events by refining rigorous checklists for every eventual-ity, then swiftly distributing them worldwide. His examples demonstrate their effectiveness: after investigating an engine failure in January 2008, Boeing developed a checklist which gave a counterintuitive instruction to pilots who found their fuel lines blocked by ice; instead of demand-ing more power, they should idle the engines for a few seconds to melt the ice. The checklist was issued in September; in November, a Boeing 777 with 247 people on board suffered the same problem, an 'uncom-manded rollback' of the engine. By following the checklist, however, danger was rapidly averted. 'It went so smoothly,' he says, 'the passen-gers didn't even notice' (p. 135). Gawande shows us that checklists are a critical tool if we want to get things right under pressure.

---

*   Atul Gawande, *The Checklist Manifesto: How To Get Things Right* (London: Profile Books, 2010).

He also examines how checklists ensure successful collaboration on complicated construction projects. Project managers are dealing with a host of contractors and subcontractors: everything they do has to fit the overall plan and be done in the right order – a day's delay in laying concrete has a knock-on effect on every other action. Extensive checklists itemise every job, who is doing it and how the work will be signed off. Gawande makes a compelling case that it is only through using checklists that tall buildings are possible – and that they have helped to bring the 'annual avoidable failure rate' of buildings down to 0.00002% per year in the United States (p. 71). The communication and collaboration checklists engender make complicated projects possible.

Most powerfully, Gawande describes his experience as part of a World Health Organisation study seeking to develop internationally applicable surgical checklists. It wasn't easy establishing what should be on the checklist or persuading skilled surgeons to use them. 'We were thrown out of operating rooms all over the world. "This checklist is a waste of time"' (p. 151). Many doctors worried checklists would undermine their professionalism, turning a highly skilled job into that of a technician. Gradually, however, they came to recognise what checklists offered: 78% of the participants in his trial saw checklists prevent surgical errors; from the trial group of 4,000 patients, 150 people avoided harm and twenty-seven lives were saved. Some 80% of medical staff who used the checklists found them easy to use and agreed they had improved the safety of care. This still seemed low to Gawande, but his last question elicited a more compelling reaction. 'If you were having an operation … would you want the checklist to be used? A full 93% said yes' (p. 157).

Gawande has marshalled a persuasive body of evidence from a range of fields suggesting that checklists offer a powerful aid to professionals – like teachers – in their work.

What makes a good checklist?

Gawande highlights a few key facets of checklists: precision, efficiency and ease of use, even in difficult situations. Rather than seeking to spell out every action, they remind users of the most important steps which even highly skilled professionals miss.

Superficially, checklists resemble shopping lists; in reality, shopping lists are to checklists as shopping centres are to umbrellas — a shopping centre covers everything and keeps us dry, but only an umbrella meets our own needs at just the right time. Shopping lists may lack order, change every week and stretch to dozens of items. Checklists are tightly targeted and designed around a specific action at a particular moment. If we wish to create a checklist, not a shopping list, we must focus on simplicity, include only a handful of items, choose the appropriate style and pause points, and build in communication.

Simplicity

Checklists should be as user-friendly as possible — neither complicated nor tricky. Simplicity may be achieved in a checklist's design or in its implementation; if a checklist isn't working, simplification is a good first response.

Seven items or fewer

Working memory is limited to roughly seven items. A shopping list can remind us of many more than seven, but the purpose of a checklist is to highlight critical actions, not everything we might do in a given situation. Bringing students' books to the lesson is crucial, writing the date on the whiteboard might be desirable; the former deserves a place on a checklist, the latter does not.

A choice of styles

We have two options:

- Check/do: We work through the list, completing each action before moving on.

- Do/check: We do everything, then check the list to ensure we've not missed anything.

Choosing between these options depends on how complicated the actions are and whether they will be completed in one go or over a longer period of time. For example, lesson resources may be collected at different points during the day and then checked (do/check), or you may work through the checklist in one go in preparation for a phone conversation with a parent (check/do).

Pause points

There is a compelling body of evidence suggesting that committing to a specific time for an action makes us more likely to conduct it.** We are more likely to use checklists consistently if we identify 'pause points' – gaps between one action and the next, often no longer than ninety seconds. My initial reaction was, 'Pause points, in a lesson – are you kidding?' I've revised my view: pause points can be created within lessons and are crucial to working effectively.

Communication

A key function of checklists in medicine is improving communication – for example, ensuring all operating room staff know each colleague's name and role makes it more likely that an individual will speak up about an error they have seen. While many teachers spend much of their time as the sole adult in the room, checklists could also be used to communicate better with teaching assistants or within teams. Some of the checklists could also improve communication between teachers and students.

** For example, 33% of students asked to write about their Christmas Eve and to submit their paper by 26 December did so (receiving academic credits in the process); of those students asked to record when and where they would write their paper in advance, 75% completed the assignment. Chip Heath and Dan Heath, *Switch: How To Change Things When Change Is Hard* (London: Random House, 2010), p. 209.

I do enough box ticking

Box ticking has acquired a bad reputation for good reasons. A tick-box approach seems particularly prevalent in schools, so it's understandable that offering teachers yet one more thing to tick might be met with suspicion.

While ticking boxes may not make us better teachers, it does not follow that following procedures harms our individuality or our professionalism. Whether in the form of a haiku, an impressive goal or a beautiful piece of music, excellence demands experimentation, originality and individual skill within a set of constraints (a poetic form, the rules of football, a genre).

Early in my teaching career I tried doing something different every lesson. It was demanding for me, uncertain for the students and incredibly wasteful of time and effort. I concluded, gradually, that my students learned best when I followed a simple lesson format most of the time, introducing experiment and excitement through the content and detail of activities. This meant that students could focus on the intricacies and interest of our topic, and not on the confusing details of the day's task. Effective, familiar structures provide a wonderful space within which we can be creative.

Another aspect of skilled professionalism is getting the details right. Checklists offer a reminder of key actions, ensuring nothing crucial has been forgotten through excitement or pressure. Even if we fear checklists may dampen our creativity – an argument I disagree with but can appreciate – it would still be worth using them to ensure everything we mean to do gets done. The accidental omission of something important has little merit as a strategy for teachers.

To give an example of the benefits of structure and reminders, the lesson planning checklist (Checklist 11) includes, 'Motive: Why is this worth doing?' This is included because I believe that, if students are expected to engage wholeheartedly in their work, I need to share something of what makes the topic useful, fascinating and worthwhile. Having chosen to write a master's essay of several thousand words on student motivation, I should need no reminder of its importance. However, while hastily planning and printing resources, I sometimes failed to include anything of the motive in lessons.

The role of the checklist was to remind me to share the motivation to learn; it was left to my skill, such as it was, to identify why the topic was of interest and how I could convey the importance of individuals' lives hundreds of years ago to teenagers today. Far from subsuming my professional judgement, the checklist reminded me to exercise it.

Many hours of my life have been spent wondering, or worrying, whether I've forgotten something important. Knowing I've completed a checklist offers another benefit: I can be confident that I've done everything I could have planned to do. That done, I can relax and trust to luck for anything not included on the checklist.

There's even a case for box ticking. Some psychological findings suggest that the act of placing a tick in a box provides a feeling of warm satisfaction, an 'efficacy boost', that makes us feel a little better about ourselves. Try it!

I have been a classroom teacher, head of department, head of professional development and I now visit great teachers for a living. I have never been an Ofsted inspector or a school improvement consultant. These checklists may help you pass an Ofsted inspection; I have no idea. They may impress your line manager; they may not. My sole purpose is to help you, as a teacher or a leader, to do your job a little better; to make your day a little less stressful and to help you get simple things right. In doing so, I hope using checklists will increase your success and boost your satisfaction.

We can all be a little bit better at what we do, every day. These checklists are one way to achieve this. I hope you find them useful.

Choose your own adventure

Checklists can work for any user – provided they clearly identify the need they seek to solve, include the right content and pinpoint the best time to use it.

This book contains a collection of checklists, loosely organised around their most likely uses: for students, in teaching, for teachers and for leaders. Many of the checklists come with examples showing how they work in practice. It concludes with guidance on designing your own checklists. So, you might choose to:

- Select a checklist you think will work for you and try using it.

- Select a checklist you think might work for you and adapt it.

- Select a checklist that echoes some of what you already do and modify it.

- Look through the checklists, think about your biggest current concern and write your own based on that.

To help you adapt checklists to meet your needs:

- You can access the checklists online at www.crownhouse.co.uk/featured/ticked-off.

- You can photocopy the checklists.

- There is space on each online checklist to add your own points.

Whichever option you choose, I would strongly suggest that you do actually use the checklist, rather than just briefly casting your eyes over it. It's all too easy to say, 'Yes, done all that. Simple.' I've found it is far better to actually check items off a list than to just tell myself I've done it – when sometimes I haven't.

This book does not pretend to offer the last word on checklists. Everything it includes is derived from techniques I've used myself or have seen tried by others. It does not include everything that matters in teaching and it does not pretend to fit the needs of your individual context precisely. It merely offers a starter kit.

At the end of the introduction to his translation of the *Oresteia*, Philip Vellacott wrote, 'The highest ideal of a translation from Greek is achieved when the reader flings it impatiently into the fire, and begins patiently to learn the language for himself.'*** In the same way, this book will have achieved its aim when the reader casts it aside, having successfully created her own checklists.

*** Aeschylus, *The Oresteian Trilogy*, tr. Philip Vellacott (London: Penguin, 1973), p. 37.

Section i

Checklists for students

The work our students do is not always as great as we hope it will be, or know it could be. I've spent whole lessons (or so it's seemed) emphasising the key features a piece of writing should include, but I've still been offered 'finished' products which lack them. I've come across students who are 'stuck' and have stopped learning entirely. I've found myself repeating the same instruction or point to individual after individual with no response. This is, no doubt, as frustrating for students as it is for me, and it's not a good use of anybody's time.

The checklists in this section are designed to address some of the reasons for such situations: uncertainty and forgetfulness among students and the plethora of demands on teachers. Checklists can help students to produce better work by providing reminders of critical elements which they can refer to at need. Consequently, students can access initial support whenever they want it, rather than having to wait their turn for the rationed attention of their teacher. They also encourage students to act more independently: they can be responsible for using checklists and improving their work themselves, rather than relying on the teacher to offer all the feedback they need.

Using them is not just a time-saving device though: checklists are a powerful tool for formative assessment:

- Checklists can show students how to do work well (particularly when used alongside model answers): as they practise using them, students gradually internalise the key features of, for example, a good paragraph or an excellent plan.

- Checklists are a swift and simple way for teachers (or students) to assess their progress: 'Show me how far you've got on the checklist.' If students are uncertain, we can redirect them to the process. If they are certain, a teacher can immediately identify a misstep; the next thing for the student to do is already there in black and white, without the teacher having to repeat it: 'Have another look at step 3 – it should go here …'

- If students are assessing one another's work, rather than the superficial feedback we often hear ('You need to write more neatly'), they can use a checklist to focus on the most important features ('You need more evidence for the point in paragraph three').

I noted in the introduction the fundamental problem that teachers face: infinite needs, finite resources. By handing responsibility for simpler tasks to students, teachers can focus on the more complicated ones: far better to use a checklist to remind a student to underline the title and spend more time discussing their struggle to describe the effect of figurative language. It also means teachers can focus their attention on students who need help most: if every student can be reminded to find the common denominator by a checklist, the teacher can concentrate on those students who have not yet grasped what this term means.

As ever, checklists won't solve all of our problems, but they can do a lot to make the classroom a more efficient, focused and productive place.

1. How do I count objects?

* Put the objects in a line.

* Touch each one as you count.

* Say the last number – this is the total.

* Challenge: Find the number card that matches.

What I love about this checklist is that it demonstrates many of the design principles of checklists in delightful simplicity. It breaks down a complicated action into its constituent, teachable parts. It provides a clear model for success. It offers a framework children can use independently when counting and peers can use it to clarify stages with one another. It is also a way for teachers to check whether students are getting lost.*

Pause point

Check/do or do/check – when counting.

How else could this be used?

A simple visual approach like this could be applied to almost any task with students of almost any age (and literacy) – for example, setting up an experiment in science, laying out materials in art or returning kit to the sports equipment store in PE.

---

* This checklist comes from Springfield School in Hackney and was first shown to me by Lucy Blewett.

2. How do I plan an essay?

* **Paragraphs:** What are the three most important points which answer the question?

* **Evidence:** Identify three strong pieces of evidence supporting each point – specific, accurate and telling.

* **Explanation:** Explain how each piece of evidence helps prove the point.

* **Mini-conclusion:** Write a mini-conclusion explaining what each paragraph has shown.

* **Rank** each reason from 1 to 3.

* **Conclusion:** Explain why reason 2 is more important than reason 3 and why reason 1 is more important than reason 2.

* **Start writing** your essay.

When students are first introduced to the idea of planning an essay it can seem dauntingly complicated. Yet mastering this process is incredibly powerful – understanding essay structures allows students to argue persuasively about any topic they know well. Simplifying the approach using a checklist can help students comprehend the process of planning an essay and the mechanics of a good essay – both what they need to do and how to approach it.

While this checklist is generic, initially I would look to make it specific to the essay topic, as in the following example. I would use it alongside a model answer which we had previously discussed. Ultimately, I hope students would internalise the structure, such that they would run through it briefly and automatically when writing under time pressure to ensure they include every aspect.

Pause point

Check/do – students read each item from the checklist, then complete that action before moving on.

When I first experimented with this approach with a Year 7 class, I was astonished to discover that pretty much every student could master the ideas underlying planning an essay – something I had spent years failing to convey to my GCSE classes.

Example

This checklist was designed to help Year 8 students answer the question 'Which historical changes most significantly affected Britain's government today?'

1.	Choose three topics for your paragraphs – write them as branches of a mind-map starting something like: *The most important change was …*
2.	For each point (paragraph), write three *good* bits of evidence. Leave a space after each one: *Henry VIII was able to use a series of laws, most importantly the Act of Supremacy in 1534, to gain control of the Church in England. (good = true, specific, detailed, with examples)*
3.	Get someone from another group to check that your evidence is genuinely strong (use the example paragraphs).
4.	Choose one bit of evidence. On your whiteboard, write how it supports your point: *Moreover, the laws enacted subsequently to clip the monarch's wings represented an end to the Divine Right philosophy articulated by James I and Charles I.*
5.	Get someone else to check that you have linked the evidence to the point of the paragraph.
6.	Explain the link from every bit of evidence and add this to your mind-map in a different colour.
7.	Write a concluding sentence to complete that paragraph: *All told, this period saw a decisive and final shift in power from the monarch to parliament, which has not been revoked since.*
8.	Get someone else to check *everything* you have already written.
9.	Start writing!

The example plan below is only partly complete, but it illustrates how this approach encourages students to pull out the key elements of an essay structure before they delve into the details.

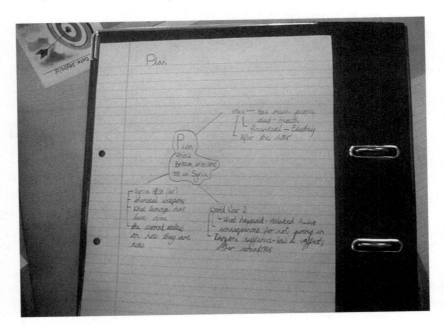

How else could this be used?

Collaboration within a group could be introduced by asking students to move a counter down the checklist one step at a time when everyone in the group has (individually) completed the step. Or students could be asked to check with a peer after each step.

Minor adjustment could adapt this checklist to other essay subjects; this same approach could work for any complicated process – for example, conducting an experiment in science or a procedure in maths.

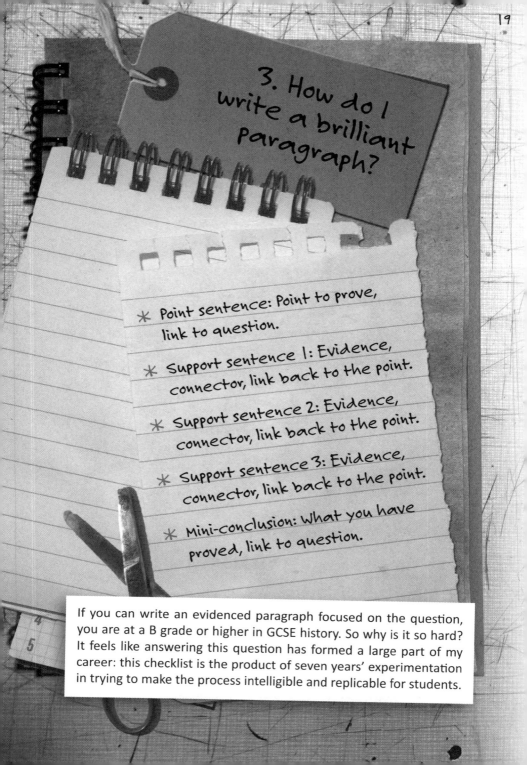

3. How do I write a brilliant paragraph?

* Point sentence: Point to prove, link to question.

* Support sentence 1: Evidence, connector, link back to the point.

* Support sentence 2: Evidence, connector, link back to the point.

* Support sentence 3: Evidence, connector, link back to the point.

* Mini-conclusion: What you have proved, link to question.

If you can write an evidenced paragraph focused on the question, you are at a B grade or higher in GCSE history. So why is it so hard? It feels like answering this question has formed a large part of my career: this checklist is the product of seven years' experimentation in trying to make the process intelligible and replicable for students.

I've never quite managed to resolve in my own mind whether it's more helpful to teach students how to plan an essay first, then how to write paragraphs, or vice versa. My best guess is that the two must be done in tandem, so this checklist and the preceding one are most productively used together. As with Checklist 2, success in this endeavour means students can use their knowledge to make a compelling argument about anything. The example below also highlights the usefulness of providing students with a model to work towards.

Pause point

Check/do – while planning or writing a paragraph; equally good as a do/check list when students think a paragraph is complete.

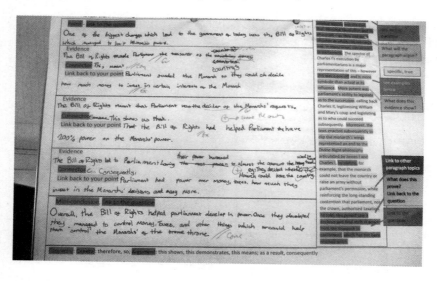

In this example, students have space to write each section of the paragraph under the checklist heading. On the right, an annotated example of a paragraph offers them a model to follow.

How else could this be used?

This checklist could be used for any form of argument.

4. I'm stuck – now what?

* Relax: Now you can learn something.

* Check the model answer: Have you included every step?

* Check your working: Is each step correct?

* Check a previous example that you've completed correctly: What is different between your previous answer and this one?

* Check teacher feedback: Are there any errors you've made recently that you might have repeated?

* Ask your peers: Can they spot your error?

* Ask the teacher.

As teachers, we hope that when students get stuck, they will keep try-ing, explore a range of ways to solve their problem and persevere to success. Too often, however, we stumble upon students sitting doing nothing because they say they are stuck and are unsure what to do. This checklist is designed to try to nudge students onto the right track with-out the teacher's help. Even while waiting, they are learning – reviewing model answers and their own work and trying different ways to solve their problems.

Pause point

Check/do – when students feel they are stuck.

> I first saw this idea in the classroom of my former colleague, Katy Sil-lem, during her NQT year. She developed it to help her deal with the problem of reaching every student, even though their needs were so diverse, to ensure they were all still learning and thinking while they waited for help.

How else could this be used?

This checklist could be amended to fit any other subject. For example, in English, we could offer a list of steps to get back on track if students lose the thread of their writing: write three possible next sentences on a mini-whiteboard, choose the best; return to the model paragraph and your plan, what have you not yet managed?

5. Is this work ready to hand in?

* Name.

* Title, underlined.

* Date, underlined.

* New paragraphs indented.

* Punctuation.

* Spelling and grammar.

* Current grammar/literacy point (whatever the student's English lessons are focusing on at present).

Version A: Is this work presentable?

One rule I follow with student work is that anything they can fix them-selves, they should. There are many aspects I might ask them to check, but this checklist collects together some essentials. In part, this gives students ownership and responsibility for improving their work. It's also a great way to increase my efficiency: it means that, when marking, I can concentrate on tricky and thought-provoking responses, since students will have corrected the simple errors.

Pause point

Do/check – on completing a first draft and before handing it in to the teacher. The checking is much better done by a peer, then returned to the first student, as they are far more likely to spot errors.

> I made a rule with a class once that I wouldn't answer questions I termed 'boring': 'What's the title?' (It's on the board.) 'What's the date?' (It's on the board.) 'Should I turn the page over?' It was a way to encourage them to make decisions and solve problems inde-pendently. This checklist extends that idea in a more systematic way to more complicated work.

Version B: Is my essay excellent?

Version B is more complicated, time consuming and demanding than version A, but it is also substantially more worthwhile. In applying this checklist to a history essay, for example, I meet many of my formative assessment goals: giving students a clearer sense of what a good essay looks like (and what an essay on its way to being good looks like), pro-viding clear explanations of the next steps and so on. The checklist is no good on its own – it rests on having previously taught and discussed the constituent parts of a good essay – but it builds on these discussions.

This checklist breaches a couple of rules (it is relatively long and has a large number of points), but it remains a checklist in spirit and function so I've included it here.

0651013

'Preflight checklist'

Name: Elia Keyn   Checker's name: Gyan .T

Checker, either:
- Ticks – if the item is present and of good quality or
- Writes the changes needed to ensure it is of good quality

	Yes/ Changed needed
	✓
Presentation	
Title (essay question)	✓
Date	✓
Name	
	✓
Introduction	
Interesting opening sentence	✓
Outline of what will be covered	✓
Explanation of why the issue is important	You need to explain why be done
Paragraph 1	
Clear topic sentence, linked to the question	✓ Also you need to add that
Evidence 1:	✓
Connective	✓
Explanation 1	✓
Evidence 2	✓
Connective	✓
Explanation 2	✓
Evidence 3	
Connective	
Explanation 3	Need to think of conn- sou
Mini-conclusion, linked to the question	✓
Paragraph 2	
Clear topic sentence, linked to the question	Needs to be a bit more powerful
Evidence 1:	✓
Connective	✓
Explanation 1	✓ but you need some here
Evidence 2	You need to work on extending
Connective	✓
Explanation 2	You need to write a bit more
Evidence 3	You need some more Explanation
Connective	✗ None, needs some improvement
Explanation 3	✗ None same
Mini-conclusion, linked to the question	✗ have same

✗ Misunderstanding Not misunderstandment   ✗ understanding.
• Perfecting that place of evidence.

Pause point

Check/do – after the first draft is completed. I ask students to check one another's work and then redraft their essays, then I mark the second draft. This peer-checking is designed to offer a fresh set of eyes on their work and provide the chance for them to learn from each other. I check with students before they begin rewriting to ensure they have worthwhile targets – for example, that no one has misunderstood the checklist and consequently given their peer unhelpful feedback.

How else could this be used?

This checklist could be applied to any substantial piece of work in any subject – for example, to check the steps of your working in maths or to verify that every aspect of an experimental report is present in science.

6. How do I draw a graph?

* Collect your equipment –
  graph paper, sharpened pencil, ruler.

* Draw x and y axes along the bold lines on the
  paper.

* Label your axes. Put the independent variable
  (the thing you're changing) on the x axis.

* Choose between a line graph (for continuous
  data) and a bar chart (for discrete data).

* Choose and write your scale. Make sure all the
  data will fit and you are using at least half
  the graph paper. Write the units along the axes,
  evenly spaced.

* Plot the points carefully.

* Draw a line of best fit (for line graphs) or the
  bars (for a bar chart).

The whole point of graphs is to illustrate data clearly. Achieving this is relatively easily done, but it requires a number of steps, each one of them critical. When we first looked at checklists in professional development sessions at my last school, my colleagues Corinne Flett and Katie Prestwich immediately saw their usefulness for graph-making. This checklist is adapted from their work.

Pause point

Check/do – each item relies on the previous ones having been completed successfully.

When colleagues met a nervous Year 7 pupil for whom drawing graphs was entirely novel, offering concrete steps to master them was a crucial support and reassurance.

How else could this be used?

A similar checklist could be created for any method that students are asked to employ regularly, whether for specific tasks (e.g. solving quadratic equations) or bigger processes (e.g. planning an investigation). The checklist could be placed alongside illustrated model answers.

7. How do I set up an experiment safely?

* Check the equipment list and identify what you need to collect.

* Decide who will collect each item, collect them and check you have everything.

* Set up the equipment according to the diagram.

* Check the experiment against the diagram – is anything missing or misplaced?

* Check with the teacher that you are ready to proceed.

Practical experiments are an important part of science, yet potentially a huge challenge for teachers. This checklist supports many aims. It frees the teacher to scan the room to ensure that everyone is focused on what they're meant to be doing. Simultaneously, it highlights the importance of a methodical approach, accuracy and safety. Yet it also encourages student independence in meeting these stipulations as well as taking responsibility for their own success.

Pause point

Check/do – each step builds on the preceding one.

> I worry about safety in science lessons because of the complexity of asking students to set up equipment in a timely, accurate and safe way. It may be residual disquiet caused by the magnesium firework my peers exploded a few feet away from my table when I was in Year 10 chemistry.

How else could this be used?

This type of checklist could be used in any lesson in which students are asked to prepare for a particular activity – for example, setting out materials in art, design and technology or food technology.

8. How do I apologise for this?

* To whom are you writing?

* What did you do? Describe it carefully.

* Why did it seem like a good idea?

* Why was it not such a good idea?

* What will you do differently in a similar situation in future?

* Sign and date your letter.

Part of the value in asking students to write their responses lies in what we can learn from them, in terms of whether they share our values or our understanding of their actions.

Here are three genuine examples from student apology notes:

'I think the school would be cool if we all broke rules because we could get into lots of fights ...'

'It benefits the school because if a visitor is coming in and everybody follows instructions more parents are going to send their children there.'

'I would like to work in a zoo ... I got a detention because I was talking at the wrong time ... Say I am holding a frightened snake, if I talk really loudly it could strike and I could die from the poison.'

Each example surprised me, each taught me something I didn't know and each demands a different response.

Sometimes, it's important we show students that a behaviour is unacceptable by giving them a detention (or whatever the school's sanction is). In the long run, however, it's substantially more important that we ask students to think through their actions (and give them the chance to explain) and commit to a different behaviour in future. Organising their thinking can be a challenge, but one solution lies in apology letters – which also provide a helpful record of students' behaviour in their own hand.

Pause point

Check/do – students should work through the prompts one by one.

How else could this be used?

The reason for asking students why something seemed a good idea, and why it wasn't one, is to help them acknowledge the reasons for an action (e.g. 'I thought it would be funny'), while showing them the choice was poor. These questions could be replaced with one question along the lines of, 'Who did this action harm?' to encourage students to think about the impact on themselves and others.

If you don't have the time to ask students to write an apology letter, this checklist could be used as do/check at the end of a conversation to ensure that they have covered all of these points in their verbal apology.

9. Is my personal statement ready?

* Make sure you have completed all the changes suggested by people who have already seen your statement. If you're not sure what they wanted you to do, go back to them and find out.

* Make sure every sentence has an example and explanation to either:

  * Show how you became more interested in your desired subject/how you came to understand its importance. For example: 'Studying atomic structure and organic chemistry have fired my enthusiasm and have helped chart my course to a chemical engineering degree.'

  * Show how you have gained/developed increasingly sophisticated, useful and transferable skills. For example: 'My ability to articulate complicated ideas and argue a case [i.e. skill] was improved through presenting research on the recent earthquake in Japan to the class [i.e. example].'

* Be specific: it sounds more interesting and more credible.

  * Don't write, 'I wrote an essay' – say what the topic was.

  * Don't write, 'I work in a shop' – say which one.

  * Don't write, 'I did stuff for charity' – name the charity and explain what you did.

* If you are struggling with a sentence, delete it and write what you can remember: you should be left with the important bits.

* Go to www.wordle.net and hit 'Create'. Paste in your personal statement. Wordle makes words big if they are used lots of times, so you might be overusing any word which is large. Go through the statement checking any words which are big – for example, are you overusing 'skills'? If so, get a thesaurus and replace some of the 'skills' with other words.

* Make sure there are no more than five uses of 'I' in the whole personal statement. (Seriously, it helps to make the sentence structure more varied and interesting.) It might help to highlight every 'I' in the document and replace as many as you can.

* Get the statement proofread by someone whose standard of English is good – a friend, relation, younger brother, older sister.

* Make sure the personal statement is under 4,000 characters and fits in the box!

The personal statement is the culmination of a student's dreams and work; it is a chance to express all their ambitions for their subject and all they have achieved so far. It can be a huge challenge, particularly for students whose successes (and future paths) lie outside the field of persuasive writing. It also represents a big challenge for teachers who need to fit in helping students with their statements around all their other duties. This checklist is designed to guide students to write a personal statement which shows them at their best.

Pause point

Do/check – before students hand their personal statement to a teacher to check.

> For two years, I was responsible for every Year 13 student's UCAS form. So, every day after school I had several students working with me, once until 9 p.m. On one evening I had twenty students in my classroom at 5 p.m. all waiting for my help. A particular low was coming in to work when ill, on a Saturday, on my birthday, because so many students needed assistance. This was long before I knew anything about checklist theory. I developed this checklist as a survival mechanism to shift the burden of simple corrections onto the students.

How else could this be used?

This checklist could be useful if given to peers to check one another's UCAS forms and to parents to provide guidance in supporting their children. Similar principles would apply to any other external piece of writing, such as letters seeking work experience or applications for competitions.

Section ii

Checklists for teaching

We often hear that teaching is not like brain surgery. I remember, in the naive early days of my career, reading this for the first time and thinking for a moment that someone was finally going to reveal the secret to teaching well. Imagine my disappointment when the author went on to note that teaching is far more complicated: the brain surgeon prepares methodically, treats one patient at a time and has extensive support. The teacher works with numerous students and is starved of time to meet their wide-ranging needs. While difficult, teaching remains stimulating and worthwhile because teachers face this range of competing pressures in every lesson.

As long as the role of the teacher includes challenging, supporting and leading diverse groups of students in their learning, it's unlikely to get any easier. So this section of the book takes another approach: it offers checklists which help to prioritise the myriad demands on teachers' time and suggests pause points to ensure we have met the most important ones. In doing so, it sets out to help teachers choose their priorities wisely, complete them successfully and accept the limits to what they can do.

Just as Section i offered reminders of key actions for students, this section does the same for teachers; the idea, therefore, is to help teachers avoid making mistakes under pressure. Writing these checklists, however, inevitably led me to prioritise those things which my experience and the evidence suggest are most critical. In this, I hope these checklists will be particularly helpful to newer teachers who may be unsure which of the many good choices and important actions to prioritise and for whom the implicit checklists of more experienced colleagues may be invisible.

10. How do I start the year?

* How can I prepare myself for a new class?

* How will I get the students into the room?

* Where will the students sit? How will the students know where to sit?

* What will I ask the students to do when they enter the room? How?

* What will I do to get the students' attention?

* What will I say to introduce myself?

* What will I ask the students to do during the lesson?

* How will I finish?

The first lesson is the best time to set the tone for the year, whether that is one of excitement, focus or challenge. This checklist is designed to ensure that we don't overlook any of the questions this opportunity poses in the excitement and apprehension of planning the details.

Pause point

Do/check – once you have planned your opening lesson.

> As my old teacher training tutor, David Cobb, used to say, 'You never get a second chance to make a first impression.'

Example

How we answer these questions is a matter of choice, depending on the tone we hope to set for the year. Here are my preferred answers: I'm aiming to convey the value of hard work, efficiency and the importance of the subject, while also showing an interest in students' lives.

How can I prepare myself for a new class?

Talk to students' head of year, or the previous year's class teacher, and learn about each student: what are their strengths? Where do they struggle? They may also be able to offer useful advice on parents – knowing whose parent is a governor and whose parents have never heard a positive word from the school before can be very useful. If you have the time, a class list and photos of the students, learning students' names before meeting them makes a powerful impression.

How will I get the students into the room?

Stand at the door, welcome the students one by one, keeping half an eye on the room inside and half on the entering students.

Where will the students sit? How will the students know where to sit?

Creating a seating plan at the start of the year sends an important message about your authority (and your organisation). I put lollipop sticks on each seat rather than expecting students to decode a seating plan projected onto a whiteboard.

What will I ask the students to do when they enter the room? How?

I write instructions on the board, asking students to write their name, subject and my name on the front of their exercise book.

What will I do to get the students' attention?

'Could I have all pens down and eyes on me in three, two, one. Thank you, good morning.'

What will I say to introduce myself?

Less is more. It's tempting to share a short life history, but it's not necessarily helpful at this stage. A brief, 'My name is Mr Fletcher-Wood and I'm excited to be teaching you history this year', followed by an introduction to the lesson's content is a good start.

What will I ask the students to do during the lesson?

Starting with some learning makes it clear to the students why they are in the classroom from the outset. It's nice, however, to add a personal touch. Writing an introduction to themselves (e.g. a life history for a history lesson) is one approach; summarising what they learned last year and their interest in the subject is another. Aim to make it easy for yourself by giving students simple tasks on which they can focus, rather than planning on spending the whole lesson teaching from the front. This provides you with a break to catch your breath and remind yourself what will happen next.

How will I finish?

Hopefully in the same calm, orderly way you began: 'Thank you very much. Books here on your way out, chairs under, off you go.'

How else could this be used?

Similar questions arise, with slightly lower stakes, with form changes and at the beginning of new units.

11. Is my lesson plan complete?

* **Objective:** What will the students know, and be able to do, at the end of the lesson?

* **Check for understanding:** How will I know what each student has learned?

* **Hook:** How does the opening task (the 'Do now') get the students interested and thinking?

* **Model:** Is it clear to the students what success looks like?

* **Motive:** Why is this worth doing (interesting, worthwhile, challenging)?

* **Focus:** What will this lesson make the students think about?

* **Access:** Can every student access the main ideas of the lesson?

* **Challenge:** How will every student be challenged by the lesson?

* **3x:** How will I ensure the students are exposed to key ideas at least three times?

There are many ways to plan lessons – for example, painstakingly developing resources, adapting an activity from a colleague or a previous year's teaching, or hurriedly pulling together ideas at the last moment. Whichever path I take, I can become so absorbed in a particular task (e.g. creating an attractive worksheet) that I lose sight of key aspects. This checklist is designed to ensure that, whatever approach you adopt, you don't overlook something critical. It incorporates crucial ideas I've learned from Robert Phillips, Dylan Wiliam, Daniel Willingham and Graham Nuthall.*

Pause point

Do/check – when you think your lesson plan is complete.

Example

In this example I have described things I might notice and changes I might make in response.

Objective: What will the students know, and be able to do, at the end of the lesson?

Examining the lesson objectives, I may conclude they involve too much content for one lesson and split them across two. I may decide that the students' actions do not focus on the objectives – that this attractive activity doesn't actually promote their understanding of the topic.

---

*   See Robert Phillips, Making History Curious: Using Initial Stimulus Material (ISM) To Promote Enquiry, Thinking and Literacy, *Teaching History* 105 (December 2001): 19–24; Dylan Wiliam, *Embedded Formative Assessment* (Bloomington, IN: Solution Tree Press, 2011); Daniel T. Willingham, *Why Don't Students Like School?* (San Francisco, CA: Jossey-Bass, 2009); and Graham Nuthall, *The Hidden Lives of Learners* (Wellington: NZCER Press, 2007).

Check for understanding: How will I know what each student has learned?

Firstly, I need to allow time for an exit ticket or a hinge question which can swiftly and efficiently capture what every student has learned. Then I will ensure that the question I'm asking is focused around the key elements of the lesson.

Hook: How does the opening task (the 'Do now') get the students interested and thinking?

History teachers call this initial stimulus material: tasks to open the lesson which introduce the topic in an arresting, intriguing way. For example, I might introduce Stalinist purges with airbrushed pictures of those sent to prison camps; when considering controversy over the British Empire, I could ask for possible reasons why Benjamin Zephaniah refused an OBE.

Model: Is it clear to the students what success looks like?

If I want the students to write an essay, I need to show them what a good essay (and a not so good essay) looks like, and work with them to identify the constituent parts of success. For example, to teach students an operation in maths, they will need to look at each step and understand how and why it works.

Motive: Why is this worth doing (interesting, worthwhile, challenging)?

I may seek to share the topic's interest or importance by inviting the students to look for similarities with contemporary situations as we begin and then ask them to make connections with those events as we conclude. Alternatively, I could highlight how the skills or knowledge we will be using come in handy elsewhere – introducing essay writing by promising that I will teach students to win any argument.

Focus: What will this lesson make the students think about?

I may ask students to create a PowerPoint presentation about Mesopotamian culture, but my main aim is that they understand history better as a result. Stipulating no SmartArt graphics, setting minimum expectations for the content or shifting presentations from digital to paper might all ensure that the students learn more.

Access: Can every student access the main ideas of the lesson?

To help every student understand and contribute to the lesson, I may need to overcome barriers in literacy: I may include more visual cues, simplified text, a joint approach to understanding the text or more frequent checks for understanding.

Challenge: How will every student be challenged by the lesson?

I want this to be challenging to those who are familiar with the topic too, so I may prepare a more tricky task using the same sources for students who need less support or offer them more difficult sources.

3x: How will I ensure the students are exposed to key ideas at least three times?

How does the introduction of the lesson highlight the key points of the lesson? How does the conclusion reinforce or build on them? If I can add in additional reiteration of key points, then I will.

How else could this be used?

Similar questions affect long-term planning (see Checklist 31).

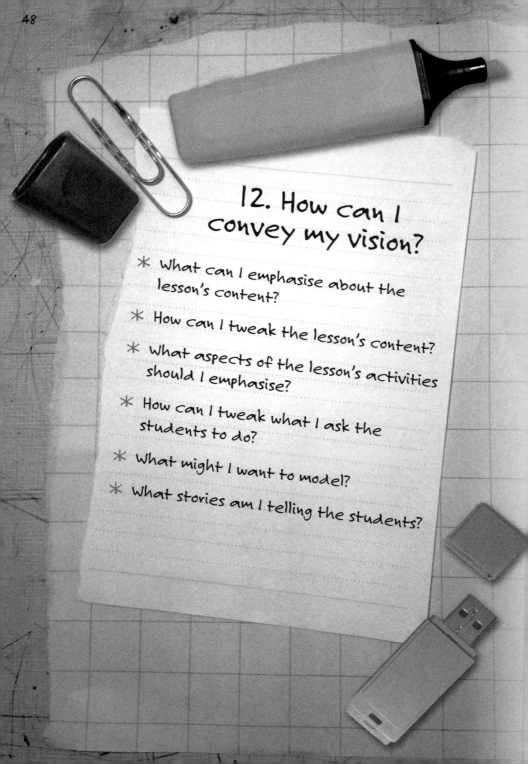

12. How can I convey my vision?

* What can I emphasise about the lesson's content?

* How can I tweak the lesson's content?

* What aspects of the lesson's activities should I emphasise?

* How can I tweak what I ask the students to do?

* What might I want to model?

* What stories am I telling the students?

Whether or not we articulate it clearly, to ourselves or others, I suspect every teacher has a greater purpose in teaching than simply helping a class to multiply fractions or use an adverbial phrase. These are important, but they are constituent parts of something bigger: fostering a joy in understanding mathematics, the ability to communicate clearly or the freedom for students to make their own choices in life. However, conveying this to students can be tricky as we can become so bogged down by the details of lessons that we lose sight of the overall aim.

Pause point

Check/do – on completing the lesson plan, but choosing only one of the changes suggested below.

The first time I planned with my vision in mind, it took me an extra hour. But I finally acted on what I'd always believed – that history could help my students understand the present better. By making explicit links between the 1923 crisis in Germany and the 2007–2008 financial crisis, I sought to show students that both have intricately linked causes and, thereby, how complex the causes of events around them are.

Example

What can I emphasise about the lesson's content?

If you want students to value scientific method, for example, and are teaching Newton's work, you could underscore the methods he used.

How can I tweak the lesson's content?

If you're teaching algebra, and you want students to value diverse cultures and religions, you might mention the achievements of medieval Baghdad. If you're teaching computing, and you would like students to value women's role in society, you could discuss Margaret Hamilton, who wrote software for the computer which made the moon landings possible.

What aspects of the lesson's activities should I emphasise?

If part of your vision is for students to have an excellent grasp of mathematical building blocks, and you're asking them to practise their times tables, you could emphasise the value of having knowledge at your fingertips. If your vision includes teaching collaboration and you want students to hold a discussion, you could highlight how much they can learn from one another.

How can I tweak what I ask the students to do?

If you hope students will value beautiful writing, you could ask them to redraft their work paying particular attention to the elegance of their phrasing. If your vision includes students learning from each another, you could ask them to give one another feedback on their writing.

What might I want to model?

If you want students to happily experiment and be unafraid of making mistakes, you could make a deliberate mistake and model the reaction you hope they would make. If you would like students to listen to and respect one another, you could show – exaggerate even – what good listening looks like.

What stories am I telling the students?

Explaining lesson activities is a great opportunity to tell brief stories which highlight those things you hope students will achieve or avoid during the task. Getting students to ask questions is a chance to mention how useful asking questions is, perhaps by mentioning the success of a former student who asked questions relentlessly. When talking to students who are struggling to behave well, you might refer to 'turnaround' students you have taught.

13. Am I ready to start the lesson?

* What resources (textbooks, worksheets, information sheets, etc.) do I need?

* What classroom supplies (paper, glue, scissors, etc.) do I need?

* Do I have student work to return?

* Are the computer and projector working?

* Have I got my lollipop sticks?

* Is there anything special to remember? Who do I need to keep an eye on? Who has been away and will need help catching up? Who struggled last lesson?

The start of the lesson has always seemed the most tense moment to me: if there is any doubt about students' mood or focus, any worries they've brought with them or any major flaw in my preparation, it is most likely to be exposed at the outset. A smooth beginning sets the tone for a solid lesson, so it makes sense to allow yourself to concentrate on students and their needs rather than whether or not you've remembered all your equipment. This is a simple, effective way to allow teachers to focus on the things that matter most.

Pause point

Do/check – a few moments before the lesson begins.

> We are three minutes into the lesson and things have started well. While students write their thoughts about the hook, I start passing out the sheets they will need next. After the first five, I realised I haven't printed enough and that the rest of the stack is with my resources for the next lesson. Cue wasted time at the laptop printing more worksheets, asking a student to fetch them and filling time while I wait for their return.

How else could this be used?

Similar checklists could be developed for the beginning of any task you regularly perform, such as assemblies, experiments and specific lessons.

14. Is the teaching assistant ready to start the lesson?

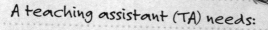

A teaching assistant (TA) needs:

* The aim of the lesson and specific aims for the students they are supporting.

* The most important two or three takeaway points from the lesson.

* The resources to hand to take a look at during the start of the lesson.

* To know who else might benefit from additional support, besides their assigned students.

* A sense of the one or two likeliest errors students might make.

* To know what students should have completed by the end of the lesson.

In an ideal world, teachers would plan lessons with TAs long in advance, or at least TAs would receive, digest and adapt lesson plans long in advance. In reality, there rarely seems to be enough time on the part of teachers or TAs, let alone a slot when both are free. This checklist would work at any stage, including a week in advance; but if such advanced planning can't be achieved, at least taking time just before or during the start of the lesson will increase the effectiveness of a TA dramatically.

Pause point

Do/check – if possible, when you complete your lesson plan; if not, check/do while students are settled on the 'Do now'.

Working in Japan as an assistant language teacher sometimes meant a day standing at the back of the room wondering what was going on and whether I might have a role to play. In some teachers' lessons, clueless as to what was going on until I watched the lesson unfold around me, I became very good at making faces at students. With other teachers, however, time to plan in advance and an invitation to participate allowed me to play a far more active role – and make lessons better and teachers' lives easier in the process.

Example

The aim of the lesson and specific aims for the students they are supporting.

'I want all students to be able to explain the three main causes of the First World War, so if the students can remember all three, then that would be a great start.'

The most important two or three takeaway points from the lesson.

'The key content is on the worksheet – for example, the tensions that existed in Europe in the early twentieth century.'

The resources to hand to take a look at during the start of the lesson.

'This is the main sheet the students will be working from.'

To know who else might benefit from additional support, besides their assigned students.

'As well as helping Anna and Alfie, I noticed that Ahmed struggled last lesson; if you could keep an eye on him and step in if he seems to get stuck then that would be very helpful.'

A sense of the one or two likeliest errors students might make.

'One thing I imagine students may get mixed up about is whether these long-term causes made war inevitable, so explain that it would be great if they could challenge this idea.'

To know what students should have completed by the end of the lesson.

'At the end of the lesson, the students will write a summary paragraph.'

'Is there anything you'd like to ask?'

How else could this be used?

This checklist could be adapted to fit various tasks, especially when you are working with a team of adults.

15. What does it take to ensure a lesson starts well?

As a student:

* I understand what I have to do to start tackling the problem.

* My emotions are managed.

* My physiological needs are met.

* I am confident that I can engage productively with the problem.

* I am motivated to try to address the problem.

* If I have more pressing problems, they are either solved or acknowledged.

* I have a safe and trusting relationship with my teacher.

* I have or can get all the equipment I need to engage in learning.

This checklist takes the idea of a good start covered in Checklists 10 and 13 and examines it from another point of view – that of the student.

Although this checklist offers a list of conditions, a healthy supply of one condition might allow for a deficit in another. For example, students with a history of positive experiences and a strong relationship with their teacher are more likely to be tolerant of unclear instructions or deliberately tricky initial tasks.

Pause point

Do/check – one helpful way to use this checklist would be asking a peer to pop into the lesson in the first few minutes to examine this for you.

> Two years ago, at a TouchPaper Problems Party, I spent an entire day puzzling over this question with fellow teachers: what are the necessary and sufficient conditions under which students will enter a classroom and most speedily engage in productive problem-solving? This checklist is the result.

Example

I understand what I have to do to start tackling the problem

If students find instructions unclear, break them into simple, sequential tasks using economical language.

My emotions are managed

If students arrive to the lesson upset, angry or worried, offer brief reassurance, remind them of their capability in the subject (or your expectations) or promise to speak to them about the issue at an appropriate time.

My physiological needs are met

If students are tired, hungry or urgently need the toilet, you may be able to solve some of these immediately and address others in the longer term.

I am confident that I can engage productively with the problem

If students feel lost on a particular problem, or have no history of success in the subject, briefly boosting their confidence or starting with easier problems (then moving on to more difficult ones) may work.

I am motivated to try to address the problem

If students are not interested in the problem, or can't see the value in trying it, brief reminders of why this topic or problem matter may be helpful.

If I have more pressing problems, they are either solved or acknowledged

If students arrive with pressing concerns that you can't address right now, promise to discuss them at an appropriate pause in the lesson or afterwards.

I have a safe and trusting relationship with my teacher

We should all be working towards this goal, but there is no short-term way to address its absence.

I have or can get all the equipment I need to engage in learning

If students lack pencils, rulers, their book or paper, provide these or remind students where they can be found.

How else could this be used?

At any transition in the lesson, a similar checklist might be useful to ensure students move into the next activity successfully.

16. Does this action merit a sanction?

* **Intent:** At a best guess, was the action deliberate?

* **Degree of disruption:** How did the action affect the student's peers or the class?

* **Persistence:** Is this the first time this lesson? First time this week? First time ever?

* **Comparison:** How did I respond to a similar action during period 1?

* **Rest of the lesson:** Had the student been working hard up until this point?

* **Possible effect:** Will giving a detention send an important message? Will it cause more trouble than it's worth?

* **Urgency:** Does this need to be dealt with now, or could it wait until the end of the lesson?

A fascinating study of judges in Israel found that the first prisoner they saw each day had around a 65% chance of gaining parole. By lunchtime, this had dropped to almost zero. After lunch, the chances were high again but they dropped even more quickly as the afternoon wore on.*

Whether due to tiredness, hunger or simply growing impatience, I'm pretty convinced that teachers suffer the same shortening of temper that judges do as the day proceeds. Certainly, I fear I'm more likely to issue a sanction rather than a friendly reminder in period 6 than period 1, even for identical student behaviour. Whether your school and classroom are strict or lenient, it's important that sanctions are consistent. Challenging behaviour usually requires a swift response, so there will never be much time available for this checklist, but it might ensure that students are treated with the fairness they deserve.

Pause point

Check/do — after a student has ceased the problematic behaviour but before speaking to them. For example, if you have asked them to step out of the classroom for a moment, use this checklist before going to speak with them.

Example

Brett gave Brian a shove when passing his desk. Brian's arm was jogged but he just turned and grinned at him. Brett is often silly at the start of lessons but appears to have turned over a new leaf recently. The school is not a strict one.

Intent: At a best guess, was the action deliberate?

Yes, definitely.

---

*   Shai Danziger, Jonathan Levav and Liora Avnaim-Pesso, Extraneous Factors in Judicial Decisions, *Proceedings of the National Academy of Sciences* 108(17) (2011): 6889–6892.

Degree of disruption: How did the action affect the student's peers or the class?

It distracted one person briefly.

Persistence: Is this the first time this lesson? First time this week? First time ever?

The first time this lesson and the third time this month.

Comparison: How did I respond to a similar action during period 1?

I sanctioned Bea when she did something similar this morning.

Rest of the lesson: Had the student been working hard up until this point?

Yes.

Possible effect: Will giving a detention send an important message? Will it cause more trouble than it's worth?

It will send an important message regarding Brian's ability to work in peace.

Urgency: Does this need to be dealt with now, or could it wait until the end of the lesson?

It should be discussed briefly now while it is fresh in Brett's mind but a long conversation is not needed at this stage.

Conclusion: the behaviour deserves a low level sanction. It was a deliberate disruption but it was limited in scale and harm.

How else could this be used?

A similar checklist could apply in other situations where you might react unfairly.

17. How will I help my students to master this vocabulary?

* What new technical terms will be introduced? How will they be introduced, exemplified and committed to memory?

* What challenging words are necessary to the text? How will they be dealt with while the students are reading?

* What unnecessary challenging words are there? Can they be removed?

* What visual support is there for key words?

* What will students do if they're stuck?

* How will students' vocabulary learning be reinforced and recorded?

Students need to understand around 90% of the words in a text to have a chance of comprehending the rest of it, so it's critical that we support them in building their vocabulary. Identifying words which are likely to be problematic, and highlighting and explicitly defining key technical terms in your subject are powerful tools to ensure comprehension.

Pause point

Check/do – when planning a new unit or lesson, and do/check once a plan is complete.

Example

What new technical terms will be introduced? How will they be introduced, exemplified and committed to memory?

This new lesson demands an understanding of *monarch, cabinet, parliament* and *prime minister*. The terms will be introduced through pictures at the start of the lesson and then returned to several times during the lesson.

What challenging words are necessary to the text? How will they be dealt with while the students are reading?

The text includes a number of other terms which may prove challenging: *representative, election* and *cornerstone*. The students will be asked to mark unfamiliar words and will then be given time to ask about them.

What unnecessary challenging words are there? Can they be removed?

On reviewing the text, *spiritual* and *temporal* add very little to student understanding and are not essential, so these words can be removed.

What visual support is there for key words?

There is a key word glossary for this unit on the walls which includes images. Pictures are also used in the PowerPoint introduction to the lesson.

What will students do if they're stuck?

There will be time to ask me and dictionaries will be available on desks.

How will students' vocabulary learning be reinforced and recorded?

The students each have their own glossary in the back of their exercise books, and they will be given time to add to it in the last five minutes of each lesson.

18. Am I meeting all my students' needs?

* Students with visual needs.

* Students with hearing difficulties.

* Students with restricted mobility.

* Students with autism or autism spectrum disorder.

* Students who speak English as an additional language.

* Students with other learning difficulties.

Special educational needs data often provide teachers with a massive amount of additional information running to many pages. A short checklist can help to identify the most important actions you need to take. Very few students conform to a 'type' of additional need: I have taught students registered with additional needs who made no use of specific forms of support, and I have met students whose teachers (or they) had found clever tweaks to support them which went far beyond those recommended in their plans. So, this is very much a checklist which requires your own intervention before use.

Pause point

Do/check — before the start of lessons.

My former colleague, Caroline Cullen, began creating checklists for the teachers of individual classes to share around the school. In doing so, she distilled the extensive advice and detail in students' personal plans into checklists which provided all teachers with the advice they needed.

Example

Students with visual needs

Text enlarged to font size 28, student wearing his glasses, right (stronger) eye facing the board.

Students with hearing difficulties

Seat the student in the front row with their stronger ear facing you, keep background noise to a minimum, give a clear visual indication of who is talking, position yourself to face the student when speaking.

Students with restricted mobility

Remove the expectation of moving around the classroom if this is inappropriate and allow the student to leave early to give them enough time to reach the next lesson, but ensure they do not miss out on key ideas as a result.

Students with autism or autism spectrum disorder

Minimise noise, maintain a consistent structure and give students prior warning about changes.

Students who speak English as an additional language

Clear, sequential instructions, adapted texts, additional prompts and visual cues.

Students with other learning difficulties

A student with dyslexia, for example, may need a coloured filter to place over text.

19. Formative assessment: is it working?

* Do students know where they're going?

    * What does success look like?

    * What are the key steps needed to achieve it?

* Do I know how much the students understand now?

    * Is my knowledge of the students' current performance accurate and timely?

* Does my feedback tell the students what they need to know?

    * What do students do with it?

* How are the students helping one another?

    * Is collaboration helping them to learn more?

* How are the students assessing themselves?

    * Is their assessment accurate?

    * What are they doing with this knowledge?

Effective formative assessment is one of the most useful tools teachers can employ and the one best supported by the evidence. Yet formative assessment frequently suffers from misunderstanding and misapplication due to the emphasis on Assessment for Learning activities rather than the underlying spirit of the techniques. This checklist is designed to help teachers focus on the key elements of formative assessment and whether or not these aims are being achieved in lessons. If not, then there is a range of techniques available to help you achieve your underlying purpose.

Pause point

Do/check – whenever you have time to review progress in the classroom or when you can invite a colleague in to offer their opinion.

> Erroneous advice about Assessment for Learning techniques came early on in my career. 'If the lesson objectives aren't on the board during the lesson, Ofsted will fail you,' was one such piece of misinformation. It was some years later that I learned about the underlying principles – like sharing the direction of the learning – which had been buried by an obsession over individual techniques.

Example

This example covers the first point in the checklist only.

Do students know where they're going? What does success look like? What are the key steps needed to achieve it?

A colleague spoke with half a dozen students and looked at their books, and found some of them did not appear to be able to explain the qualities of a good essay. Considering the underlying purpose of sharing what students are aiming for, I could:

- Share model 'excellent' and 'quite good' essays and work with students to break down what makes them excellent or good.

- Share an essay planning, or paragraph writing, checklist (like Checklists 2 and 3).

- Briefly assess their work (either individually or as a class), picking out one or two key next steps which would help them to write better and then discuss them next lesson.

How else could this be used?

Students could be asked to complete the checklist for you.

20. That lesson was a disaster – now what?

* At what point did the lesson begin to unravel?

* What was happening beforehand?

* What happened, or what was missing, when the lesson did unravel?

* What was the underlying cause(s) of the problem?

* What can I do to address the underlying cause(s)?

* What one thing could I change next lesson?

* How (if at all) should I discuss this with the students?

* Wipe the slate clean and move on.

Our instinct after a dreadful lesson may not be to sit and evaluate exactly what made it so bad, but it is important that we make the time to do so. Identifying problems and their causes can help us to find ways to fix them before we encounter them again. From an emotional perspective, focusing on these solutions enables us to evaluate our qualities as professionals and to learn from the process; if we don't do so, we are likely to keep replaying the lesson in our minds for the foreseeable future. Being able to wipe the slate clean after a bad lesson or bad day is a key habit of successful teachers in challenging schools.

Pause point

Check/do – at the first available pause after a disastrous lesson.

> I went home one day in my first year of teaching upset about a lesson with my Year 10 class. I worked that evening. I woke up in the morning, still angry, and reached my next lesson with the class still feeling resentful. The moral I took from this was not to work in the evenings: a good one. A more productive moral I failed to appreciate at the time was the importance of analysing the disaster constructively and making a plan to fix it.

Example

At what point did the lesson begin to unravel?

On moving from the hook, which had worked well, into the main task.

What was happening beforehand?

Students were discussing the hook and speculating on what it suggested about the lesson question.

What happened, or what was missing, when the lesson did unravel?

I asked the students to begin reading the text and writing their responses, but some students didn't do as I'd asked.

What was the underlying cause(s) of the problem?

Superficially it appeared to be the behaviour of some of the students. But, in fact, I think my instructions weren't very clear and the students didn't have sufficient knowledge to approach the text competently.

What can I do to address the underlying cause(s)?

I could focus on changing my seating plan but, more importantly, I need to ensure that the introduction to the lesson provides the prior knowledge the students need to approach the main part of the lesson.

What one thing could I change next lesson?

Include a quick review of the relevant points from the previous lesson before starting the main section of the lesson.

How (if at all) should I discuss this with the students?

I don't think this needs talking through as it's a simple change. As we begin, I'll flag up that we'll briefly review the relevant points that have already been covered as this should make the main task more approachable.

Wipe the slate clean and move on

I am still a competent teacher. I had one bad lesson with a few students. I have formulated a way to fix it and my other lessons went well. And, anyway, I'm seeing friends this evening.

How else could this be used?

This checklist could work equally well as a framework, either for a mentor to structure a conversation or for a teacher to talk through a disastrous lesson with a colleague to gain some useful advice.

21. Are students ready for exams?

* Do the students know the dates of their exams?

* Has the course been completed leaving enough time for revision?

* Have the students been taught explicitly and practised the skills they will need to deploy in exams?

* Do the students have revision materials?

* Do the students know revision strategies?

* Do the students understand how the marking criteria apply?

* How will the students who have been absent for a long time be supported?

* Do the students have good plans for the day itself (e.g. last minute revision, equipment, settling strategies)?

Andy Day, a fantastic former head of faculty at Withernsea School, has written insightfully about some of the reasons why students may struggle in exams. He describes this checklist, one of the first he drew up, as being a way to ensure that the mechanics of preparing students for exams is fully diagnosed and deconstructed.* Providing an aide memoire for subject heads about appropriate best practice proved a salutary way of highlighting ways of working that should be routine for all departments, but weren't being implemented. The checklist helped to repair these lapses.

Andy explained to me:

> There was a significant variation in exam results between subjects at my school – more than we felt should exist. So, what were the subjects getting the historically higher grades doing that the others weren't? We worked backwards from the student, sitting in the exam hall and facing their paper, backfilled all the necessary subject knowledge, understanding of exam technique, skill in using the available time to their best advantage and so on. This methodical approach supported all departments to achieve high grades.

In constantly striving for improvement, Andy observes that we frequently embellish the way we teach our students from year to year – finding a new technique here, inserting a new piece of insight into how the grading works there. But if we're not careful, we can forget the more obvious and routine things that we had been doing before which worked well. It's a case of celebrating the new but not permitting the old to simply evaporate.

Andy says: 'Checklists are a way of making sure we that maintain a focus on good, grounded practice from year to year; adjusting as necessary but making sure that the key nuts and bolts are regularly rehearsed and polished.'

---

* Andy Day, Piloting a Surgical Approach to Checklists, *Meridianvale* (24 November 2013). Available at: https://meridianvale.wordpress.com/2013/11/24/piloting-a-surgical-approach-to-checklists/.

Pause point

Check/do – the return from the Easter holidays.

How else could this be used?

Similar checklists could be built around coursework or controlled assessments.

Section iii

Checklists for teachers

Section ii provided checklists designed to make teaching easier and more effective. This section moves on to look at the vital aspects of teachers' work and lives which go on behind the scenes.

In some ways, the checklists in this section are for actions conducted when you are under slightly less pressure – they are about meetings, preparation, reviewing and so on. However, we are just as prone to forgetfulness and oversight in the process of our work as we are in the classroom, so small tweaks are equally likely to make our days, weeks or terms more efficient and our lives slightly easier.

What life outside the classroom may lack is clear boundaries between one activity and another, or between one lesson and another, so finding ways to create and mark out pause points is even more important.

22. What should I achieve this week?

* What are the three most important non-urgent actions I can complete in each of my roles this week?

* What one unimportant but unavoidable action will I complete this week?

* When will I fit in each action?

* What other pressures might I need to plan around this week?

* Saying no: To whom and how?

* Sense check: Is this feasible?

How can we possibly do all the things we want to do as teachers? I base my answer on Stephen Covey's work on time management.* He invites us to divide our tasks up into the following four categories (I have given examples for each category):

i. Urgent and important	ii. Not urgent and important
Fight in the corridor	Planning next term's unit
Planning your lesson for period 2	Getting to know your form better
Answering your head teacher's angry email	Identifying strategies to improve as a teacher
iii. Urgent and unimportant	**iv. Not urgent and unimportant**
Some emails and requests	Complaining!
Some conversations	Some emails
Some administrative tasks	Some administrative tasks

In schools, I would add a fifth category: unimportant and unavoidable – for example, some data analysis, Ofsted readiness and internal accountability tasks.

Covey argues that the most successful people spend most of their time working on things found in quadrant ii. Given the examples I've used above this makes sense: if you have planned and resourced a unit in advance, individual lessons are less of a challenge. Taking time to build relationships with students makes it more likely that you can identify and prevent incipient trouble. Ensuring that documents are up to date, obligations are fulfilled and communication with the head is good makes it less likely that she will walk into a classroom or meeting and be surprised (and unhappy) with what she sees. In short, the more time spent in quadrant ii, working on long-term issues which build towards success, the less it is necessary to firefight unexpected problems and crises.

Covey advocates setting out to complete three tasks in each of our professional roles each week. These roles might include: teacher, form tutor,

---

* Stephen R. Covey, *The 7 Habits of Highly Effective People* (London: Simon & Schuster, 2004), p. 151.

head of department, newly qualified teacher, Key Stage 3 coordinator and so on. This checklist is designed to help make that process routine.

Pause point

Check/do – on Friday afternoon or Monday morning, as you work out what the week will look like. Then do/check with the list you create during the working week.

There are numerous tips out there on saving time as a teacher, but tactics like clever folders don't address the need to juggle a raft of lesson preparation, teaching duties, Ofsted readiness activities, preparing for trips, leading continuing professional development and getting ready for an external departmental review. Fundamentally, we have to limit and focus our efforts.

How else could this be used?

A similar planning checklist could apply to the term or the year.

23. How can I protect my well-being?

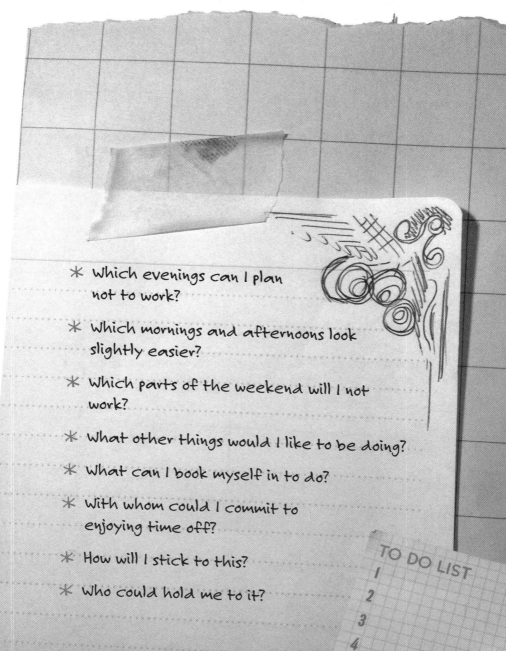

* Which evenings can I plan not to work?

* Which mornings and afternoons look slightly easier?

* Which parts of the weekend will I not work?

* What other things would I like to be doing?

* What can I book myself in to do?

* With whom could I commit to enjoying time off?

* How will I stick to this?

* Who could hold me to it?

TO DO LIST
1
2
3
4

This checklist is best used in conjunction with how we plan for the week (Checklist 22). This proceeds from the assumption – indeed, the habit – of many new and experienced teachers that they will be working every evening and every weekend. I would challenge the wisdom of this assumption, but if you do hold it, or if your friends and colleagues do, then this series of steps may help you to find and maintain the space to do other things.

Pause point

Check/do – as you plan your week or at the point when you realise you are about to overdo it this week.

I developed this checklist through watching an impressive coaching conversation between a colleague, Dan Monaghan, and a Teach First participant, as he coached her into planning ways to look after herself.

How else could this be used?

This checklist could equally well be used to frame a conversation with a colleague who is struggling to look after themselves.

24. How do I make an idea sticky?

* Simple: What is the core idea?

* Unexpected: What makes the idea surprising?

* Concrete: What details bring the idea to life?

* Credible: Where does the teller's authority lie?

* Emotional: How does the idea tug at our heartstrings?

* Stories: How can the idea be encapsulated in a story?

* S (the last 's' in the acronym SUCCESs is, regrettably, spare).

Chip and Dan Heath's first book, *Made to Stick*, sought to explain why some dodgy ideas stick (like students' credence in the influence of the Illuminati), while more worthy ideas (sun cream is important) can get lost.* They summarise their key ideas by marshalling the evidence into a simple mnemonic: SUCCESs. If you want to make essential content in a lesson memorable, using some of their suggestions may help.

Pause point

Check/do – when designing a sticky message for a lesson.

Example

When planning a lesson on Magna Carta, I might consider:

Simple: What is the core idea?

The king bows to the will of his subjects for the first time.

Unexpected: What makes the idea surprising?

How can the king possibly be inferior to others? Or, what would make people so angry that they rebel against their king?

Concrete: What details bring the idea to life?

We picture the rebel barons sitting down with King John at Runnymede, the king's anger and his sealing of the charter.

Credible: Where does the teller's authority lie?

I could call on Churchill as an authority: 'Here is a law which is above the King and which even he must not break. This reaffirmation of a supreme

---

*   Chip Heath and Dan Heath, *Made to Stick: Why Some Ideas Take Hold and Others Come Unstuck* (London: Arrow, 2007).

law and its expression in a general charter is the great work of Magna Carta; and this alone justifies the respect in which men have held it.'**

Emotional: How does the idea tug at our heartstrings?

I might tap into the fear of arbitrary arrest and punishment: 'Imagine that you could be locked up, and left there, never having the chance to have your say.' Or, to stick more closely to the theme, I could ask students to imagine being so angry that they rebel against their legitimate ruler.

Stories: How can the idea be encapsulated in a story?

The lesson content already provides a story. I could choose to tell it as a story or allow it to emerge in stages during the lesson.

How else could this be used?

A similar approach can be taken when designing key messages for students, whether conveying our vision for what we hope students will achieve and why their work matters, or simple tutorial messages about ways they can look after themselves.

** Sir Winston Churchill, *History of the English-Speaking Peoples*, Vol. 1: *The Birth of Britain* (London: Cassell, 1956), pp. 256–257.

25. How should I read research?

* What does the research claim?
* Where was the study published?
* How directly does the study's method deal with the study's topic?
* How many people were in the research sample?
* Was there a control group?
* How statistically significant were the effects?
* Has this study been replicated elsewhere?
* What do other studies say about it?
* Does it fit my context?

As more teachers seek to inform their practice by research, and to keep up with the latest studies, a research checklist seems like a good idea. This won't make your reading of the analysis perfect – a brief checklist is no substitute for deep reading and study – but it may help you ask some of the critical questions which will ensure you pinpoint the key issues.

Pause point

Check/do – when you finish reading a piece of research, or do/check before you make any statement which begins, 'The evidence shows ...'

Example

Raj Chande, Michael Luca, Michael Sanders, Xian-Zhi Soon, Oana Borcan, Netta Barak-Corren, Elizabeth Linos, Elspeth Kirkman and Sean Robinson, Curbing Adult Student Attrition: Evidence from a Field Experiment, Harvard Business School Working Paper, No. 15-065 (February 2015).

What does the research claim?

Text messages designed to help students feel motivated, plan their attendance or connect with one another increased their attendance at college by 7% and reduced the likelihood that they dropped out of their courses by 36%.

Where was the study published?

It is a 'working paper', so it has not been peer reviewed.

How directly does the study's method deal with the study's topic?

The method was to send text messages to students and monitor their attendance, so it couldn't be much more direct.

How many people were in the research sample?

The study involved 1,179 students – enough for this to be considered a serious trial and reduce the likelihood of chance factors affecting the outcome.

Was there a control group?

Yes, the sample were split in half between the 'treatment' group who received the text messages, and the 'control' group who didn't. There was a random selection process to determine who received the messages and who didn't. The researchers were also careful to divide people randomly between the treatment and control groups by whole classes, to make it less likely that a message to one person would affect someone else in the same class who hadn't received the message.

How statistically significant were the effects?

Most of the effects were significant at the $p < 0.01$ level. This means it's very likely the results were due to the effects being tested for in the study and were not due to chance.

Has this study been replicated elsewhere?

No, but it builds on other studies in related fields.

What do other studies say about it?

Nothing – yet …

Does it fit my context?

My school has an automated text message service for parents, but it bans students from bringing their phones into school. So, the research might be relevant if there was a system to get messages to parents in a way that didn't come across as patronising.

26. How can I get this past the head?

* What am I asking for exactly?

* What are the costs?

* Why is it important for me?

* Why is it good for the students and the school?

* How can I minimise the negative impacts?

* How can I maximise the gains?

* What are the counter-arguments? Why don't they apply in this case?

Bodil Isaksen suggested the value of this checklist and it appealed to me immediately: sooner or later, as a teacher, you are likely to end up in front of your head of department or head teacher, asking them to do something novel, counter-intuitive or costly. You may be asking to get parents into the school, to take students on a trip, to go on an expensive course or change structures within your department. Whether you find yourself approaching an easy-going leader keen to develop and retain you or a harried warrior with a reputation for being difficult, this check-list is designed to give you the best chance of demonstrating that your idea is a good one.

Pause point

Check/do – before knocking on the head's door.

Example

What am I asking for exactly?

I'd like to attend an expensive course on formative assessment.

What are the costs?

The cost of the course and the cover that will be needed.

Why is it important for me?

This will be excellent professional development for me.

Why is it good for the students and the school?

Formative assessment is a priority for the school and getting an up-to-date and expert picture of it will be of great benefit to all teachers.

How can I minimise the negative impacts?

I can swap my duties on that day with colleagues; I will also highlight any other advantages the day has such as fewer lessons or no exam classes.

How can I maximise the gains?

I will spread what I learn in the training to colleagues through professional development sessions.

What are the counterarguments? Why don't they apply in this case?

We have two other teachers absent. However, this is a relatively light teaching day for me.

27. Am I ready for my job interview?

* Does the lesson plan explain what I will be doing at each point in the lesson, and why?

* Do I have all the necessary lesson resources?

* What is the school's vision, ethos and context?

* Why do I want this role? Why would I be good at it?

* What are my key strengths in my current role? What evidence supports this?

* What would I do in a child protection case? (This is a question you are almost certain to be asked, and yet I know people who've been caught out by it. Hint: tell the designated child protection officer.)

* How will I get to the school early?

No checklist, however good, can prepare a teacher so well that they are assured of getting the job for which they are applying. However, this checklist will ensure that you're not missing anything critical and, hopefully, it will act as a nerve settler to help you get a decent night's sleep before the interview.

Pause point

Check/do – the weekend (or evening) before the interview.

It may seem ridiculous but for my last interview I had planned different ways to get to the school on time if each of the tube lines I needed was closed. I *really* wanted the job ...

How else could this be used?

With a handful of adaptations, this checklist would be suitable for any job interview.

28. How can I have a useful conversation with parents?

* Why am I calling?

* What result am I seeking?

* What data will I use?

* What data might I be asked about?

* What is the parent like? What is their relationship with the school like?

* How will I address the parent?

* What's in my script?

Parents and carers can be powerful allies; conversely, if they conclude that you're not working in their child's best interests, they can be problematic opponents. If you need support with students, parents are often best placed to give it. While the wishes of most parents overlap with the wishes of most teachers, their views as to how this can be achieved, and their list of priorities, may differ. Some parents may have had negative personal experiences with schools and some may have had many years of negative phone calls from their child's school. So, calling a parent for the first time is cause for both optimism and a slight degree of apprehension.

Pause point

Check/do – before lifting the receiver.

Example

Why am I calling?

While you might want to say, 'To vent about how annoying Malcolm was in my lesson' or 'To update Malcolm's mum', a narrower focus is more likely to be a good use of your time, and the parent's, and lead to a more useful outcome. For instance, the reason for your call might be, 'To share Malcolm's recent test result, express my concern, and ask for assistance in helping him to improve his work'.

What result am I seeking?

A productive conversation is likely to lead to some sort of agreement and action, even if that is simply to ask the parent to pass on your praise. Do you want the parent to check Malcolm's book each day? To speak to Malcolm about how he's doing? To ground him all month?

What data will I use?

Whatever you're discussing, you want the evidence at your fingertips. In this case, what test result did Malcolm get, and how does that relate to his last test? How many times have you had to ask him to leave the classroom? Exactly who threw what at whom? Having the evidence to hand allows you to make a much more convincing case to the parent.

What data might I be asked about?

You may want to talk about Malcolm's behaviour, but this is Malcolm's parent's chance to discuss everything he's done this year with you. It's worth having your mark book to hand and briefly reviewing how he's done across the year.

What's the parent like? What's their relationship with the school like?

It's worth asking your colleagues for information about the parent's relationship with the school, past experiences and simply when would be a good time to call. If your school data management system runs to it, find out how often the parent has heard from the school.

How will I address the parent?

Again, some data management systems cover this, but if you can't pronounce the student's surname it might be worth practising. If there are any doubts, 'Is that Malcolm's mother?', may be easiest.

What's in my script?

Writing a script for your first few lines can help you think through what you want to say and how the parent might respond. For example, 'Hello, is that Malcolm's father? It's Mr Fletcher-Wood, his history teacher, do you have a moment to talk? I just wanted to call because I've been quite concerned about Malcolm's progress. In his last test he only reached a D, although we're targeting him a B. And I actually had to ask him to leave the class this morning ...'

How else could this be used?

The principles behind this checklist make it suitable as a basis for conversations with colleagues, particularly if you anticipate a disagreement.

29. Am I ready for parents' evening?

* Books: Marked and up to date.

* Data: Handy in my mark book or printed out from the student information system.

* Water.

* Coordination with colleagues if classes are shared.

* Appointment list.

* Who to get hold of in case I need a senior colleague's support.

* Opening lines, key points, closing lines.

Evenings spent speaking with parents and carers can be great fun, but like phone calls home they can also be very challenging. Ensuring that you are well prepared for parents' evening, even if it's just little tabs in your mark book to flick between different classes, can make life significantly easier. It can also invest your remarks with the additional authority of centralised school-wide data.

Pause point

Check/do – in preparation for a parents' evening, or do/check just before the evening starts.

Section iv

Checklists for leaders

Just like teachers, school leaders are under pressure to make difficult decisions with limited time. The biggest difference is that the impact of a leader's decision is more far wide-ranging and (depending on the school) more likely to face immediate and determined opposition.

In the same way that the distinction between checklists for teachers and leaders is open to debate, so this section contains a number of checklists which teachers as well as leaders may find useful – leading a trip and creating a scheme of work are two obvious ones. They are collected here, however, because these checklists address actions which demand leadership, such as requiring collaboration from fellow teachers and leading other adults.

30. Have I been inducted properly as a middle leader?

* Meetings:
    * What is the agenda?
    * Who chairs them?
    * What is the follow-up?
* Finance:
    * What resources do we have and need?
    * How do we order things?
    * How do we follow up on those orders?
* Schemes of work:
    * Where and how do we plan schemes of work?
    * How do we use them as a department and as individuals?
    * When and how do we review them?

* Exams:

  * Who is responsible for exam entries and how?

  * Who performs the results analysis?

  * Who deals with exam returns?

* Interventions:

  * What interventions do we run?

  * Who attends?

  * What's the follow-up for individuals and for analysis?

* Department plan:

  * How is the department plan developed each year?

  * How is the plan used?

  * When and how is the plan reviewed?

* Culture:

  * How do we do things around here?

  * What's special about the department and the team?

  * What do we not do?

Handovers between outgoing and incoming leaders may take many forms – it may be rushed or even non-existent if your predecessor has already left. Moreover, when new to a post you often don't know what questions to ask until you're confronted by a particular situation, by which time your predecessor may have moved on.

This excellent checklist, suggested by Andy Day, is designed to ensure that a middle leader has been inducted properly. He developed it because he was concerned that schools often make a new appointment and then effectively throw the appointee in at the deep end. The school leadership is then disappointed when they struggle.

Andy argues that an effective induction programme should be the result of widespread discussion, a clarification of the key skills the role entails, an assessment of the level of competence required and assigning an experienced 'buddy' or mentor to ensure the plane lands with its under-carriage down and the wheels spinning.

Pause point

Check/do – during an induction conversation, or do/check at the end of it.

> My first induction to take over a new role within a school was with a colleague who was leaving teaching at the end of the summer term. I wrote down everything he said in slightly rushed note form. By the time I was in post in September, I was sure he (or, more likely, I) had missed some key points but by then he was in a new job elsewhere.

How else could this be used?

An equivalent induction checklist could be designed for new teachers by departments or pastoral teams.

31. What does a unit of work need?

* Knowledge: What is the substantive knowledge the students should remember from this unit?

* Threshold concepts: What deep developments in understanding (i.e. irreversible changes in the way the students see the world) might this unit lead the students in to?

* Assessment: How will we know if the students have learned what we hope they will learn?

* Vocabulary: What words must the students know to make sense of this unit?

* Links to prior knowledge: What previous topics and existing understanding does this build upon? How can we revisit them for the students who have missed out on it?

* Links to the curriculum: What is this unit preparing the students for?

* Links to other subjects and to life: How does this unit help the students to understand other subjects and the world?

Although we tend to focus our concerns on short-term issues before we consider long-term issues, effective planning works the other way round. Individual schools and departments often have their own preferred ways of planning units, but this checklist is designed to focus attention on the aspects which are most critical to a scheme of work.

Pause point

Check/do – while planning, or do/check once the scheme of work is completed.

Example

The example to the right is an early draft (the assessment is summarised in a separate document) for part of a Year 8 history curriculum.

Unit guiding question: why don't we agree on the British empire?

By the end of this unit you will be able to …	By the end of this unit you will be able to explain the meaning of …	You may pass through the following threshold concepts (in no particular order) …
Bronze • Name five countries taken over by the British • Describe specific features of each country • Name five ways the British gained power and give an example country for each • Name five reasons why the British wanted an empire • Name two positive effects and two negative effects of being part of the Empire **Silver** • Explain the commemorative plate's interpretation of the Empire • Explain Zephaniah's interpretation of the Empire • Explain Ferguson's interpretation of the Empire	These concepts: • Bias • Colonisation • Empire • Free trade • Interpretation These words: • Britannia • Censors • Colonise • Communication • Conspire	That the British Empire has positive and negative effects on individuals and societies. The way people felt about and reacted to the Empire was differentiated according to nation, race, class, gender and other factors. (Crude national/racial categories do not explain how people felt about the Empire.) That the same thing can be portrayed in many different ways, with a degree of accuracy.

continued

By the end of this unit you will be able to ...	By the end of this unit you will be able to explain the meaning of ...	You may pass through the following threshold concepts (in no particular order) ...
continued • Explain the Mau Mau War Veterans Association's interpretation of the Empire • Explain Nairobi's interpretation of the Empire **Gold** • Explain why the commemorative plate's designer interpreted the Empire like this • Explain why Zephaniah interpreted the Empire like this • Explain why the Mau Mau War Veterans Association interpreted the Empire like this • Explain why Nairobi interpreted the Empire like this **Platinum** • Explain how interpretations come about and are constructed and how we can approach and evaluate them	• Contrary • Elite • Gulag • Imperial • Import/export • Jubilee • Lure • OBE • Portray • Poseidon/ Neptune • Tame • Trident	That the way an interpreter portrays something may be affected by their background, intended audience, the evidence available to them and by contemporary concerns. That simple assumptions about the effects of an individual's background on their interpretation can be deceptive. That using terms such as 'us', 'they' and 'we' can obstruct us from studying history well. That every interpretation is biased in some way – so the term 'biased' in isolation is unhelpful.

32. How can I make a meeting work?

* **Aim:** What do I want to achieve through holding the meeting?

* **Attendance:** Who actually needs to be present to achieve this aim?

* **Preparation:** How can people arrive best prepared? How can I make it easy for them to complete this preparation?

* **Catch-ups:** How will I provide colleagues with sufficient time to catch up and share recent successes and failures, without allowing this to take over the meeting?

* **Agenda:** Is there a logical flow? Are we dealing with the most important and contentious issues first? How long will we spend on each item?

* **Debate:** How will I encourage discussion and debate when I need to canvass a range of opinions?

* **Follow-up:** Who will do what? By when?

An honest, if somewhat flippant, response to the question, 'How can I make a meeting work?' comes from Jason Fried: 'If you do have a meeting coming up, if you have the power, just cancel it. Just cancel that next meeting.'* He describes meetings and managers as the two biggest drains on productivity. If it is desirable to bring together a group of colleagues for a meeting, this checklist is designed to ensure that the experience is productive and worth your time.

Pause point

Do/check – the afternoon before the meeting.

Example

Aim: What do I want to achieve through holding the meeting?

Moderate A level coursework.

Attendance: Who actually needs to be present to achieve this aim?

All teachers who have A level coursework classes this year, our trainee who will be teaching A level classes next year and the head of department as an experienced A level marker; no one else.

Preparation: How can people arrive best prepared? How can I make it easy for them to complete this preparation?

Colleagues need to have marked at least three pieces of coursework by students who they expect to be near the top, middle and bottom of the

---

* Jason Fried, Why Work Doesn't Happen At Work, *TED.com* (2010). Available at: http://www.ted.com/talks/jason_fried_why_work_doesn_t_happen_at_work?language=en.

range. I sent a reminder at the start of the week and will send another one this afternoon in case anyone needs to do this at the last minute.

Catch-ups: How will I provide colleagues with sufficient time to catch up and share recent successes and failures, without allowing this to take over the meeting?

Five minutes to talk through getting the coursework in, then remind everyone what time the meeting is due to end.

Agenda: Is there a logical flow? Are we dealing with the most important and contentious issues first? How long will we spend on each item?

Start with the middle pieces as the most contentious and the area where most of the work will fall – so, twenty-five minutes for the middle, fifteen for the top and ten for the bottom.

Debate: How will I encourage discussion and debate when I need to canvass a range of opinions?

Ask everyone to read through and make notes without speaking for the first few minutes of each section. Go round and get judgements, without comment initially, then open up the debate.

Follow-up: Who will do what? By when?

All colleagues to complete marking by 31st and confirm they have done so by email. Further moderation meeting if there is serious disagreement.

How else could this be used?

This checklist could be used for planning any meeting between adults.

33. How do I design a powerful CPD session?

* Objective: What will teachers be able to do by the end of the session?

* Outcome: What will teachers make or do by the end of the session which will show what they have learned?

* Hook: How will I get teachers' attention and communicate the importance and validity of the session?

* Links to reality: How does this link to the school's priorities? How does it relate to teachers' day-to-day concerns?

* Research: What validates the approaches I am advocating?

* Contextualisation: What does this look like in maths? In science? In a range of year groups?

* Practice: Time for teachers to put suggested changes into action and allow them to sink in (see Checklist 34).

* Feedback: What did teachers make of the session?

* Follow-up: When and how will teachers be asked to use what they've done, and report back on how it went?

This checklist is part of a pair: this one sets out the overall design principles for a continuing professional development session, and the next one
(Checklist 34) outlines the key features of the practice part of the session.
The checklists can be used separately (for example, you might run a CPD
session which does not adopt the practice methodology described in the
next checklist), although I would suggest they are best used together.

The choices in this checklist are designed to achieve two things: firstly,
to ensure that teachers have a worthwhile and useful experience; and,
secondly, to ensure the value of the session is communicated to teachers swiftly, overcoming any thoughts of other priorities or negative
experiences of previous sessions. It owes a lot to the teacher learning
communities model advocated by Dylan Wiliam.*

Pause point

Check/do – in designing the session, or do/check once complete.

> As a teacher, there's always something else you could be doing, and
> this is likely to be weighing on you as you enter a professional devel-
> opment session. The temptation to do a bit of marking or answer the
> odd email during the session may be very strong for busy colleagues.
> Showing them immediately that there's a reason not to is key.

Example

*Objective: What will teachers be able to do by the end of
the session?*

Use the formative assessment technique of increasing their wait time
before and after student questions.

---

*   See Dylan Wiliam, Content Then Process: Teacher Learning Communities In the
    Service of Formative Assessment, in Douglas Reeves (ed.), *Ahead of the Curve: The
    Power of Assessment To Transform Teaching and Learning* (Bloomington, IN: Solution
    Tree Press, 2007), pp. 183–204.

Outcome: What will teachers make or do by the end of the session which will show what they have learned?

Teachers will practise using longer wait time in small groups.

Hook: How will I get teachers' attention and communicate the importance and validity of the session?

Tell an anecdote about being told that I should increase my wait time by a student, the depth of student responses this led to and my guilt at realising how much I'd been missing out on.

Links to reality: How does this link to the school's priorities? How does it relate to teachers' day-to-day concerns?

Links to school's priority of improving oracy and the teacher's priority of ensuring every student gets a good chance to contribute.

Research: What validates the approaches I am advocating?

Introduce the findings of Tobin's (1987) literature review.**

Contextualisation: What does this look like in maths? In science? In a range of year groups?

Give examples of when it might, and might not, be worth increasing wait time (e.g. some kinds of questions and for particular pupils).

Practice: Time for teachers to put suggested changes into action and allow them to sink in

Teachers role play waiting longer before and after student responses.

** Kenneth Tobin, The Role of Wait Time in Higher Cognitive Level Learning, *Review of Educational Research* 57(1) (1987): 69–95.

Feedback: What did teachers make of the session?

Allow time for teachers to put forward their views.

Follow-up: When and how will teachers be asked to use what they've done, and report back on how it went?

Teachers commit to a given time to use this strategy, and a time when a colleague will visit them and see it at work.

How else could this be used?

Many points from this checklist would apply when introducing new policies to staff.

34. How do I design an effective practice session?

* Objective: What skill (or part of a skill) will teachers master by the end of this session?

* Success points: What differentiates being great at this skill from being good?

* Practice: What practice activities will teachers do to achieve this mastery?

* Preparation: When and how will teachers prepare what they will say and do in their practice?

* Model: How will I show teachers excellence in the skill? How will I show them excellence in the practice activity?

* Feedback: How will I ensure teachers receive constructive and useful feedback?

* Integrate or loop: What will I do to increase the challenge if teachers succeed initially? How will I reduce it if they struggle?

* Enduring change: How will teachers synthesise and record what they will do with what they have learned?

* Culture of practice: Looking back through the plan, how will I build in opportunities to make practice feel important, safe and fun?

This checklist is adapted from the Teach Like a Champion team's Practice Perfect workshop, and the book which shares the rules of their practice.* Influenced by them, I have come to believe that professional development only leads teachers to change if it goes beyond inviting them to consider what good teaching is and offers them the chance to put it into practice there and then.

Pause point

Check/do – while designing the session, or do/check when you have completed your plan.

Example

Objective: What skill (or part of a skill) will teachers master by the end of this session?

By the end of the session they will be prepared to plan effectively by formulating accessible, challenging and meaningful objectives.

Success points: What differentiates being great at this skill from being good?

Economy of language, specific (measurable) objectives and alignment to the curriculum.

Practice: What practice activities will teachers do to achieve this mastery?

Teachers will work from the curriculum plan to identify the knowledge inherent in a curricular objective, choose one section of that knowledge and formulate appropriate lesson objectives.

---

* Doug Lemov, Erica Woolway and Katie Yezzi, *Practice Perfect: 42 Rules for Getting Better At Getting Better* (San Francisco, CA: Jossey-Bass, 2012).

Preparation: When and how will teachers prepare what they will say and do in their practice?

Teachers will write their lesson objectives from the curriculum.

Model: How will I show teachers excellence in the skill? How will I show them excellence in the practice activity?

I will talk teachers through the process of creating lesson objectives from the curriculum, giving examples from maths, biology and physics. I will also emphasise what not to do (i.e. choose activities first and then find lesson objectives to fit).

Feedback: How will I ensure teachers receive constructive and useful feedback?

Teachers will pause in their objective writing halfway through, share objectives with someone teaching the same subject and offer feedback to each other. I will offer three possible lines to help focus their feedback (be more specific, reduce the amount of material and increase your economy of language). I will also model applying this feedback with a poorly framed objective.

Integrate or loop: What will I do to increase the challenge if teachers succeed initially? How will I reduce it if they struggle?

To integrate, I will ask teachers to begin planning the assessment they would use to evaluate whether the lesson objectives have been met; to loop back, I will ask teachers to focus back on the knowledge implied by the curriculum and identify a single objective teachable in a lesson.

Enduring change: How will teachers synthesise and record what they will do with what they have learned?

Teachers will write one short-term and one long-term takeaway, and note when they will act on it.

Culture of practice: Looking back through the plan, how will I build in opportunities to make practice feel important, safe and fun?

I will model how I accept and use feedback myself, to demonstrate that feedback need not feel threatening. I will also share some of my own protracted failures honestly, and the errors of judgement I made which caused them.

How else could this be used?

This checklist could be used for any activity when teachers want their students to practise to achieve mastery.

35. Is the trip ready to go?

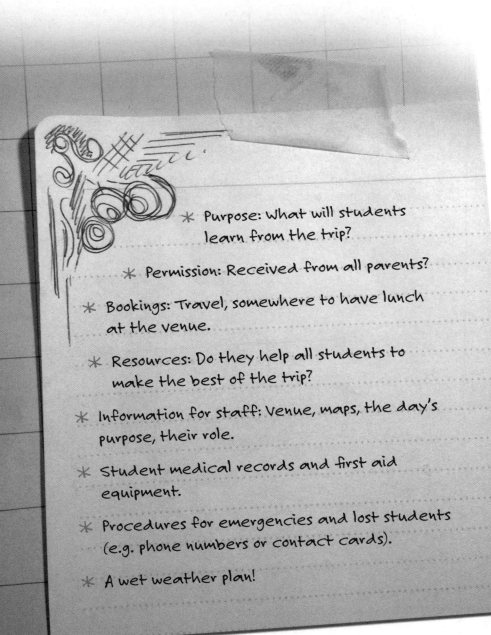

* Purpose: What will students learn from the trip?

* Permission: Received from all parents?

* Bookings: Travel, somewhere to have lunch at the venue.

* Resources: Do they help all students to make the best of the trip?

* Information for staff: Venue, maps, the day's purpose, their role.

* Student medical records and first aid equipment.

* Procedures for emergencies and lost students (e.g. phone numbers or contact cards).

* A wet weather plan!

Well-designed trips are an amazing opportunity for students to experience another world, bring learning to life and expand their horizons. Ill-designed trips are a tedious waste of time for students and an exhausting ordeal for staff seeking to corral them and minimise public complaints. This checklist is designed to help you ensure that your school trips fall into the former category.

Pause point

This checklist can be used either as a check/do in planning (allow a few weeks at least), or a do/check reassurance the day before.

> Brief moments of terror I have faced during trips include realising I'm missing: (a) a student, (b) tickets for my group, (c) shelter for a hundred students on a rainy day and (d) seventy children and four teachers, last seen heading in the wrong direction in the Science Museum.

Example

Purpose: What will students learn from the trip?

Students will revise and strengthen their understanding of historical periods by visiting important buildings from each era in central London.

Permission: Received from all parents?

Check the list and call any parent who has not completed the form.

Bookings: Travel, somewhere to have lunch at the venue

Travel booked with Transport for London and tickets received; entry booked with the one site they will visit; nowhere to have lunch but have shared with staff a list of suggested places they could shelter if it's too cold to eat outside.

Resources: How do they help all students to make the best of the trip?

Booklet with a series of questions for students designed to encourage them to look hard at key points; treasure hunt activity. Students will return to the school an hour before the end of the day to be quizzed on what they've learned.

Information for staff: Venue, maps, the day's purpose, their role

Copies of maps; email sent to all staff previously; staff will attend the student briefing and there will be time for me to explain the itinerary to them.

Student medical records and first aid equipment

With me and group leaders.

Procedures for emergencies and lost students

All students have a card printed with the school contact details to use if they become lost.

A wet weather plan!

Change order of venues to reduce distance covered outside.

How else could this be used?

Similar considerations apply when visitors perform or run workshops at your school.

36. What am I looking for in this observation?

* Classroom culture: Are the students focused on learning?

* Objectives: Is there a clear purpose to the lesson? Do the lesson activities promote that purpose?

* Direction: Are the students clear about what they are doing and how to do it well?

* Access and challenge: Are all students able to engage in the lesson? Are all students challenged?

* Assessment: How does the teacher assess student understanding before, during and after the lesson? How is this used in their teaching?

* Specifics: Are there particular telling moments and examples which it would be helpful to discuss?

Observations are troublesome beasts: they can be a powerful tool for teacher improvement, yet there is also worrying evidence that observers' impressions of lessons can sometimes align poorly with student progress. Either way, observations remain the most commonly used form of individual professional development that teachers receive, so it pays to use them wisely.

The priorities given here are based on the assumption that the goal of the observation is to help the teacher improve their practice. Depending on how long the observer spends in each classroom, they may not see every aspect in one lesson. The priorities identified combine some of those highlighted in the leverage observation process used by Uncommon Schools* and some aspects of formative assessment. Checklist 37 sets out ways to approach feedback.

Pause point

Check/do (or, in this case, check/look) – during an observation.

---

37. How do I give useful feedback?

* Praise: What has the teacher done particularly well? How did she go about doing this?

* Probe: What aspect of the lesson do I want to focus on? What did the teacher notice about that phase?

* Explicit target: What do I want the teacher to try changing about her practice?

* Practice: How can we turn the idea of change into reality?

* Reinforcement: How can the change be practised further to ensure a degree of fluency?

* Plans: When will the teacher use this? When will I see her again? When will we next meet?

If observing can be tricky, the next step – providing feedback that engenders change in the observed teacher – is even harder. The most common response to feedback is to leave practice unchanged. Often this is because the way feedback is given evokes a defensive response from teachers. Sometimes it is because the targets they are given are too numerous or unclear. However, even if the teacher accepts and wishes to use the feedback, they may still go away and find that they are too busy in the business of planning or teaching to use it.

Simple tweaks to the format of feedback, again based on the Uncommon Schools approach, can make feedback genuinely useful. This example sets out what an observer would say and do.

Pause point

Check/do – before the feedback meeting begins.

Example

Praise: What has the teacher done particularly well? How did she go about doing this?

'We set a target of doing a quick check for understanding for all students, so you could be confident you were ready to move on and I was very happy to see exactly that. What has the impact of these checks for understanding been?'

Probe: What aspect of the lesson do I want to focus on? What did the teacher notice about that phase?

'What was the point of the check for understanding?'

'What did you learn from doing it when you did?'

'When might it have been more powerful?'

(Here you are seeking to elicit that the check for understanding would have been most useful before students started the written task, allowing them either to gain additional support or skip the task entirely and go on to the next activity.)

Explicit target: What do I want the teacher to try changing about her practice?

'I would like you to plan "hinge questions" at points in the lesson which will help you decide how to proceed.'

Practice: How can we turn the idea of change into reality?

'So, what I'd like to do now is look ahead to a lesson when you will use the hinge questions. Where would they fit best? When do you need to know what the students know? What will you do if they all get it? What will you do if none of them get it? What will you do if five of them don't get it? What will you do if only five of them get it?'

Reinforcement: How can the change be practised further to ensure a degree of fluency?

'Can we have a look at another lesson ...?'

Plans: When will the teacher use this? When will I see her again? When will we next meet?

'When I come in next week, I'll look forward to seeing that work.'

How else could this be used?

Similar principles could be applied to any feedback given to colleagues.

38. How should I use this data?

* **Validity:** Does this data actually reflect what we are using it to measure?

* **Reliability:** If we ran a similar test again, would we get a different result?

* **Interpretation:** How else could we interpret this data?

* **Limitations:** What does this data not show?

* **Context:** What other data or information sheds light on this issue?

* **Choices:** What would I do differently if I didn't have this data?

School leaders often seem inundated with data. They then seek to ground their decisions on that data: how to group students, which teachers to assign to which groups, whether or not teachers are performing well and so on. Yet sometimes, in the process, limited or problematic data is invested with an unearned authority, leading to potentially ill-advised decisions. In his book, *What If Everything You Knew About Education Was Wrong?* David Didau suggests that checklists are a good way to respond to this danger.* This checklist is adapted from his suggestions.

Pause point

Check/do – before making any decisions using the data.

Example

The winter teacher assessments for Year 9 students are being used to consider what options the students will be allowed and encouraged to take at GCSE.

Validity: Does this data actually reflect what we are using it to measure?

Teacher assessments may not reflect students' aptitude for GCSE – for example, if teachers only tested a small part of the curriculum for this entry, it may not reflect students' overall attainment in this subject.

Reliability: If we ran a similar test again, would we get a different result?

Teacher assessments are not particularly reliable, especially if they were not moderated.

---

* David Didau, *What If Everything You Knew About Education Was Wrong?* (Carmarthen: Crown House Publishing, 2015).

Interpretation: How else could we interpret this data?

The data appear to show that students are doing far better in French than in German, which would suggest we should create more French than German groups. Are there other reasons that might explain this – for example, the relative difficulties of the language, how long students have been studying it or who is teaching the course?

Limitations: What does this data not show?

This data tells us nothing about student or parental choice. It doesn't tell us very much about how students may change during the rest of the year. In some subjects, progression from Key Stage 3 to GCSE may move at different speeds.

Context: What other data or information sheds light on this issue?

Could we ask students about their likely choices? Could we ask parents about their hopes for their children? When we made this decision last year, how did it work out? The year group for whom we made this decision three years ago have now received their results. What were the consequences for them?

Choices: What would I do differently if I didn't have this data?

I would be working on what our school believes matters for our students' futures, what parents believe and what the students wish for. Is there scope to consider these in more depth?

How else could this be used?

This checklist could be used any time when we seek to take action based on available data.

39. How can I make a difficult conversation manageable?

* Scenario: Where and when will I find time to speak with my colleague?

* In line: How will I introduce the topic and set the tone?

* Probing questions: How will I learn about their perspective?

* Vision: What underlying purpose am I trying to convey?

* Action: What concrete thing do I want them to do, and when?

* Follow-up: What will the next steps be, and when will we meet again or talk next?

'Difficult conversations' may be a cliché, but questions about them are a staple of leadership interviews for a good reason: sooner or later, it will be your responsibility to initiate a difficult conversation. This checklist is influenced by Stephen Covey's fifth habit of highly effective people: 'Seek first to understand, then to be understood'.* It also focuses on the importance of having and conveying a positive vision to the rest of the leadership team.

The blogger @ImSporticus has adopted checklists to help manage conflict as a head of department. He explained:

> There comes a time when conflict needs to be confronted and resolved. If it doesn't credibility and trust drops which has a massive negative impact not just for all those involved, but others that are close to them as well, either professionally or personally. Using checklists has helped me to begin to take the steps out of my comfort zone, depersonalise conflict where possible and keep the discussion around the issue and explain how we together intend to manage it.

Example

Scenario: Where and when will I find time to speak with my colleague?

Approach them at around 4.30 p.m. when their revision class will be over and they will have had a chance for a short break.

In line: How will I introduce the topic and set the tone?

'Is now a good time to talk?' If yes, sit down facing them. 'I wanted to understand what you said yesterday about the new curriculum.'

---

* Covey, *The 7 Habits of Highly Effective People*.

Probing questions: How will I learn about their perspective?

'I was curious what you meant when you said you didn't think Year 8 could manage this kind of content. Why do you think they would struggle? What do you think would cause the biggest difficulties?'

Vision: What underlying purpose am I trying to convey?

'We agreed that we needed to revise the curriculum to ensure the students are ready for the new GCSEs. Do you agree with that principle? In which case, we will need to prepare students better, earlier.'

Action: What concrete thing do I want them to do, and when?

'I would love to get your help on reviewing the Year 7 curriculum so students are ready for Year 8.'

Follow-up: What will the next steps be, and when will we meet again or talk next?

'Could you take a look at the Year 7 curriculum, and can we meet to discuss what you've noticed next Tuesday?'

How else could this be used?

Similar principles may fit with some individual conversations with students.

40. How can I make behaviour change easy?

Make the change:

* Easy:

  * Shrink the change: How can I make the change seem (and be) small and achievable?

  * Script the critical moves: What's the first step of the change?

* Attractive:

  * Find the bright spots: Where's it going well? How can I build on this?

  * Find the feeling: What's the emotional appeal?

  * Provide goals: What's the long-term direction?

* Social:

  * Grow your people: How do students' own identities push them towards the change?

  * Rally the herd: How can I make it seem like the change is already dominant?

* Timely:

  * Tweak the environment: How can I design the context of an individual's choice to promote the desired change?

  * Build the habit: What actions could be used to trigger repetition of the change?

How do we ensure students reach lessons promptly? Most schools struggle with incentives, silent corridors and registers, but Chip and Dan Heath offer another example: put a sofa at the front of the classroom.* They describe students racing to lessons to get the 'cool' seats, which just happen to be in the front row. This may not be practical or scalable, but it's a good example of the benefits teachers can obtain from looking at problems through the lens of behavioural psychology and 'nudges'.

Pause point

Check/do – in designing a change, or do/check when we're not happy with the way students (or colleagues) are behaving.

Example

Shrink the change: How can I make the change seem (and be) small and achievable?

'Look, the first two are done for you – keep going from there' or 'Just write two sentences' are powerful starts and give students instant small wins. Immediately follow up with, 'OK, that's great – now give me two more lines.'

Script the critical moves: What's the first step of the change?

Instead of asking a distracted student to 'focus' on a fantastic seminar, I told her I wanted her to ask one brilliant question before the end of the session. Her hand flew into the air.

Find the bright spots: Where's it going well? How can I build on this?

In a challenging class, look at the students who are focused and moti-vated. What's motivating them? How can they be role models?

---

*   Heath and Heath, *Switch*, p. 187.

Find the feeling: What's the emotional appeal?

A maths teacher once told me that he would promise his students they would never be lied to if they did well in his classes, tapping in to their desire for autonomy.

Provide goals: What's the long-term direction?

I have pictures of history graduates in a range of careers on the wall and a pie chart showing all the professional destinations of Cambridge history graduates.

Grow your people: How do students' own identities push them towards the change?

How can we tap into students' pride and their affiliations to family, school or neighbourhood? Ask, 'What would a really thoughtful person do in this situation?'

Rally the herd: How can I make it seem like the change is already dominant?

'Great start from Andy' and 'Good thoughts written down by Jem already' show which way the lesson is going.

Tweak the environment: How can I design the context of an individual's choice to promote the desired change?

I want students to be able to look at the board and listen to me, and also to speak to one another in most lessons. Neither rows nor group tables allow me to do this, but L-shaped tables do.

Build the habit: What actions could be used to trigger repetition of the change?

Ask students to write down what time they will do their homework.

41. How can I keep staff happy?

* **Model:** How have I modelled that well-being matters?

* **Red line:** What red lines have I promised? Which promises have been broken?

* **One in, one out:** What additional demands have I made? What demands have I taken away in return?

* **Autonomy:** What have I given staff control over? What else could I give them control over?

* **Mastery:** How have I helped staff to improve their work?

* **Purpose:** How have I reminded staff of our aims and achievements?

There are school leaders out there who don't believe staff well-being is important or is a priority; there are some who believe that 'We're doing it for the kids' and that's sufficient. Bluntly, I would counsel no one to work for anyone who takes such a view. Far more common are leaders who want to ensure staff well-being is good but who struggle to uphold this commitment in the face of myriad other pressures.

This checklist is designed both for planning in advance and, perhaps more powerfully, for the point at which leaders realise that things have slipped, as a way to review what is and isn't working. It's based, in part, on Daniel Pink's work,* and is an acknowledgement that some aspects of staff well-being are about motivation as well as conditions.

Pause point

Do/check – when a teacher comes to you worried about their well-being or at a set point in the year.

How else could this be used?

In planning well-being strategies for the year.

---

* Daniel H. Pink, *Drive: The Surprising Truth About What Motivates Us* (New York: Canongate, 2009).

42. How can I make this initiative work?

* **Rationale:** Why am I doing this – for students, for parents, for Ofsted?

* **Preparation:** How has this been tested, piloted and consulted on?

* **Clarity:** How have the procedures and expectations been simplified so they are easy to follow?

* **Sweetener:** If I am making a big demand, what existing tasks can I remove or fold into this request to maintain reasonableness and proportion?

* **Model:** How will teachers see leaders putting this into practice?

* **Launch:** When should everyone start? By when should they finish?

* **Accountability:** How will teachers be held accountable?

School leaders are applauded for their new initiatives far less frequently than they introduce them. Sometimes, important new ideas are met with hostility and seen as unnecessary and unwelcome burdens. On other occasions, a lack of clarity as to what is expected can lead teachers to not follow the new expectations. (For example, my own lack of certainty as to the point at which students are expected to be silent has caused me to struggle to implement school behaviour policies.) And at other times, the absence of accountability means that initiatives are dropped before they go any further. (For example, when I was instructed to colour code every single seating plan for all my classes with every additional student need I got bogged down, but when I realised no one was checking I stopped worrying about it.)

This checklist is designed both to help leaders check that the initiative is a good idea and limit the opposition they may face in implementing it.

Pause point

Check/do – in designing an initiative, and do/check before mandating its use.

Section V

Checklists for living

In writing this book, I developed a number of checklists which seemed useful but could not be described as being for teachers directly. I debated removing them, fearing I might stray unwittingly into long-distance life counselling – something I lack any right, wisdom or desire to do. However, late in the writing process, Bodil Isaksen shared with me a checklist she had formulated (Checklist 46: How can I make this school day a good one?). I was reminded that the true value of checklists lies not in the advice they offer, but in the reminder to do the things we already know we should do that they provide. The checklists in earlier sections reflect situations I've experienced: I've missed key aspects of lesson preparation in my haste; I've seen teachers forget the limitations of assessment data due to pressures from leaders. If we can fall into these traps, we can certainly overlook wise responses when we're emotional, exhausted or under pressure. With this in mind, I hope teachers, who spend too much of their time in these states, will benefit from these final four checklists.

43. How can I get this decision right?

* Widen your options:

  * What would I do if I had none of my current options?

  * Who else has solved a similar problem?

* Reality test your assumptions:

  * How can I challenge my current way of thinking?

  * What's the average success rate for people who've made the same decision I have?

  * How can I pilot my idea?

* Attain distance before deciding:

  * How will I feel in ten minutes, ten months, ten years?

  * What is my long-term goal?

  * Take a pre-mortem: It's a year on, the decision was a disaster – why?

  * And a pre-parade: If this is an overwhelming success – then what?

* Prepare to be wrong:

  * What tripwire will cause me to rethink my choice?

* Make the process feel fair:

  * How can we reach a decision collectively?

  * How can I show the fairness of the decision-making route I have taken?

Alongside *Made to Stick* and *Switch* (see Checklists 24 and 40), Chip and Dan Heath's work also includes *Decisive,* a book with the beguiling subtitle, *How To Make Better Choices In Life and Work.** In it they offer a series of tools to help us think through the decisions we're making fully and come to better conclusions. These tools have inspired this checklist.

Pause point

Check/do – in thinking through a decision, or do/check when you're struggling to decide.

Example

At some point in their career, most teachers will wonder whether it's time to leave their first school for pastures new. Between the uncertainty of moving outside the environment in which they have trained and the fear of staying in one place for too long, this process can become circular.

Widen your options

The choice is not simply stay or go. There are many options: stay for different periods of time, go to many different kinds of school, leave teaching for a while (or forever), look for roles within the school which fit what you want to do and so on.

Reality test your assumptions

Visit other schools and talk to friends who are a year or two ahead in the process – how do they feel about their move?

---

*   Chip Heath and Dan Heath, *Decisive: How To Make Better Choices In Life and Work* (London: Crown Business, 2013).

Attain distance before deciding

What are you aiming towards? Are there particular fields of teaching in which you wish to specialise? What are the benefits of staying or moving on? Why might this go wrong?

Prepare to be wrong

What will you do if you hate your new school? What will you do if you decide to stay longer at your current school and then feel it's the wrong decision?

Make the process feel fair

If you have a good relationship with close colleagues and your line manager, talk your options through with them so they understand what you're seeking to do and why.

44. Have I walked myself into a trap?

* What are the underlying causes of the problem I'm trying to solve?

* What evidence have I collected about these causes?

* Have I sought opinions and evidence to contradict myself?

* When has this been tried elsewhere, and what was the result?

* How much have I sunk into this? If I was starting from scratch, would I choose differently?

* It's not either/or: What other options are there?

* What else will this lead to – positive or negative?

* It's a year on, this has failed – why?

The more I learn about psychology, the more I recognise how prone I can be to deluding myself, and how often good results derive more from luck than judgement. However, psychology also offers a few tools which, used appropriately, may help reduce our tendency for self-delusion. This checklist is adapted from questions in David Didau's book, *What If Everything You Knew About Education Was Wrong?*

Pause point

Check/do – late in the decision-making process.

Example

Marking is uneven across books from different departments, so a whole school marking policy is to be introduced.

What are the underlying causes of the problem I'm trying to solve?

If marking is uneven, are some teachers or departments focusing on other forms of feedback? Are some teachers struggling with their workload? Are some teachers working very hard but prioritising other aspects of teaching? If any of these are true, are there better ways to tackle this?

What evidence have I collected about these causes?

Was my conclusion made on the basis of a couple of book looks, or was a genuine sample of students' books made? If so, what proportion of books showed what features?

Have I sought opinions and evidence to contradict myself?

Have I asked heads of department from a range of subjects whether this will work for them? Have I asked those who seem most hostile to the idea why they are unreceptive?

When has this been tried elsewhere, and what was the result?

Have I asked other school leaders whether similar policies have worked for them? (If they have, they may be able to save you from pitfalls.)

How much have I sunk into this? If I was starting from scratch, would I choose differently?

Is it the case that the school has been trying to do this for years? Or that I announced the idea in a meeting and don't feel I can go back now?

It's not either/or: What other options are there?

It's not a case of a new marking policy or not. How about professional development sessions on marking? Sharing best practice weekly by email? Making marking and exchanging books a regular item on department meeting agendas? What about a set of marking principles to be applied differently by different departments?

What else will this lead to – positive or negative?

Will this tempt teachers to mark more during lessons but diminish the quality of marking (or lessons)? Will it tempt teachers to stick to the letter of the policy but seek other ways to reduce their workload?

It's a year on, this has failed – why?

Lack of support? Poor implementation? No accountability? Unsuitability of the policy? None of this necessarily means the marking policy was a bad idea, but it might indicate that it was not the best solution.

45. I have made a terrible mistake – now what?

* Damage limitation: How can I stop the situation from getting any worse?

* Damage repair: What can I fix?

* Apology: How will I show I am sorry?

* Prevention: How can I avoid this situation recurring?

* Learning: What can I learn from this situation? How can it help me to become a better teacher, leader or person?

* Moving on: How can I assuage my guilt and move on?

Mistakes are inevitable. My one time art teacher, Miss Thomas, used to refer to the importance of the 'happy accident', and many wise people – notably Ed Catmull at Pixar and Doug Lemov in *Teach Like a Champion** – trumpet their value. Catmull says he 'came to think of our meltdowns as a necessary part of doing our business, like investments in R&D'. He also emphasises that, while we could see this approach as implying that we should 'accept failure with dignity and move on. The better, more subtle interpretation, is that failure is a manifestation of learning and exploration.'** The question is not whether we make mistakes but how we respond. Mistakes are a fount of useful learning.

Pause point

Check/do – as soon as you realise you've made a big mistake.

How else could this be used?

This approach could usefully be taught to students too.

---

* Doug Lemov, *Teach Like a Champion: 49 Techniques That Put Students On the Path To College* (San Francisco, CA: Jossey-Bass, 2010).

** Ed Catmull with Amy Wallace, *Creativity, Inc. Overcoming the Unseen Forces That Stand In the Way of True Inspiration* (London: Bantam Press, 2014), pp. 108, 109.

46. How can I make this school day a good one?

* Realistic: Is what I am setting out to do today achievable? If not, what should I cut?

* Plans and priorities: Have I allowed time for my top priorities in school? (see also Checklist 22)

* Time for myself: At what point today will I do something nice for myself?

* Social time: When will I spend time with, or in contact with, friends?

* Exercise: When will I exercise?

* Buffering: How can I plan compensations around points of the day I know will be stressful?

This checklist is adapted from one created by Bodil Isaksen, as a way to ensure that she looked after herself during the school day. It takes the excellent principle of seeing the day as something that can be planned for, and around, so we do what we can to ensure that, whatever it throws at us, the result is a good one.

Pause point

Do/check – at the beginning of the day or the end of the previous one in preparation for the next.

Section vi

Design your own checklist

Section vi is designed as the keystone of the book. I very much hope some of the individual checklists prove useful or help you rethink or reprioritise your work. However, every situation is different – or at least feels different – and the best person to create a checklist fitting their context is the user.

This section seeks to reveal the five pillars supporting the creation of a checklist – pinpointing the problem; identifying the key elements; establishing the pause point; building in communication; and reviewing, refining and routinising – allowing you to design and then make use of your own checklists.

Pinpoint the problem

What situation do you hope to address? What error do you wish to prevent? What improvement do you want to make? What is at the root of the problems you face? How would the situation look if everything had gone perfectly? Focusing on a limited problem is likely to be more helpful than dealing with all of it – for example, ensuring students are focused when moving from the carpet to their seats for independent work is achievable; improving student focus is vaguer and therefore harder to solve.

My first checklist: the problem

I want to ensure that I am ready and organised at the start of my lessons. I have to move around between several classrooms and some of them aren't set up for history teaching, so I sometimes find I'm partway into the lesson and I'm missing a key resource.

Identify the key elements

What is critical to success in this situation? What errors are common or likely? How can the key elements be broken down into simple steps? We are not seeking a list of everything which is desirable or helpful in teaching; rather, we want to identify the critical components of success (as opposed to those which are nice to have but inessential). If you're not sure what's important or what gets missed, ask your colleagues for some suggestions.

My first checklist: key elements

The biggest issue is the specific resources for a lesson: worksheets or information sheets without which teaching can't go ahead. Other issues crop up frequently too – for example, not having lollipop sticks, making sure PowerPoint is booted up and ensuring I have enough lined paper for students to write on. So, the key elements are: my resources, generic resources, marked work to return, PowerPoint, lollipop sticks and anything special for this particular class.

Establish the pause point

When will you use the checklist? A perfectly designed checklist used at the wrong time is useless. Given how busy the school day can be, finding the right pause point at which to use your checklist is key.

Do you want a do/check or a check/do list? Will it be more helpful for you to do everything and then check you've done it properly (do/check) or go through the list one item at a time and tick off each item as you go (check/do)?

Where will you put the list? Placing the checklist somewhere noticeable and convenient may remind you to use it.

My first checklist: the pause point

The best time to check is shortly before the start of each lesson, just when I have everything lined up for that particular lesson – any earlier and I'll leave something for later; any later and I won't have time to improve on what I do. I normally organise things at different times (my lollipop sticks will start off in my folder, students' work on my desk and the sheets at the printer), so the best thing to do is gather everything up and check when I think I'm ready. But I still need to leave enough time to do whatever I've forgotten or I'm missing, so preferably about five minutes beforehand. As I'm moving around a lot, it's hard to think of anywhere to keep a checklist, but I will incorporate reminders to use the checklist into my plan for each day.

Build in communication

How can the checklist promote communication? Nurses are more likely to raise problems they spot during operations if everyone introduces themselves at the start of the procedure (a checklist item). Teachers do not generally work with new people on a regular basis, but the checklist still has a role to play in improving communication. With whom do you need to communicate, and what checklist item guarantees that you will do it? Is there an apt moment to share your lesson plan with your teaching assistant? Do you want to ask students to communicate particular issues with you at certain times?

How can creating the checklist promote communication? If the checklist is to be used by more than one person, then dropping a finished product (however well-designed) into their lap may not evoke the reaction you anticipate. Sitting down with the intended users and asking, 'What should go on this checklist?' makes the checklist part of a common endeavour, and your colleagues may well suggest points you have overlooked. It may also prove a helpful opportunity to talk through and clarify what you think is important – for example, asking students to think about what should be on a checklist for a particular piece of work may offer a useful lesson in, or reminder of, what a good piece of work requires.

My first checklist: communication

Since my first checklist was designed for my own use, this didn't prove relevant. However, in retrospect, I could have added something designed to build communication with a teaching assistant, when I had one. Even something small would have helped – for example, collecting one of each sheet to hand to them on entry would have sent an important message. In constructing the checklist, I could have asked the students what they noticed was forgotten most frequently in lessons. In doing so, I would have been enlisting them in the effort to make the classroom a better and more efficient place.

Review, refine, routinise

First attempts to create checklists rarely lead to the desired results. It's worth repeating Gawande's line from *The Checklist Manifesto*: 'We were thrown out of operating rooms all over the world. "This checklist is a waste of time"' (p. 151). If we anticipate this response from the start, then it may help to book a time to sit down with colleagues (or students) to consider how the checklist works, discuss what's included and when you're going to use it. If the checklist was designed collaboratively, it would be worth taking it back to the group who designed it.

My first checklist: review

When will you conduct the review?

I reviewed the checklist's effects on a daily basis during the first few days I was using it. I assembled the mistakes I saved myself from in the first few days of using a checklist. Without the checklist, I would have:

- Failed to check individually on a couple of students I was meant to.

- Left the (dry and uninspiring) lesson question unchanged.

- Printed out the sheets I needed but left them on the printer.

- Omitted to reorder my PowerPoint slides, leaving me flicking in the wrong direction and confused.

- Failed to print out spare sheets for students I knew had been away.

- Left a lesson unchanged (and again failed to print resources) and taught it to a second class, even though it had confused the first group I'd taught it to.

My first checklist: refine

How will you refine your checklist? What can be removed? What should be added?

In the event, I refined my actions (for example, finding a better way to store my lollipop sticks) rather than the checklist.

My first checklist: routinise

How will you make use of the checklist routine? Perhaps the biggest barrier to adopting checklists is the belief that we're doing fine as we are. So, how can you build the use of a checklist into your routines so that it becomes something you always do – like putting the tea bag into the cup before adding hot water?

Keeping a list of the errors I'd avoided showed me the value of what I was doing. After the last catch on the list above, I stopped recording the errors I was avoiding and instead routinised the use of checklists. I've been tempted to omit its use on a number of occasions, particularly when I'm in a hurry. (It's at these moments when I'm far more likely to have missed something critical to the lesson, which a sixty second pause would allow me to establish.) I need to keep working to normalise using a checklist, so that failing to use it becomes an active decision to break with my habit. I'm also trying to train myself into checking things physically rather than mentally: the mental check that I have printed out something is no assurance that I've actually collected it – indeed, I have checked once, checked twice and still failed to pick something up.

Conclusion

The list of things checklists won't help you with is, sadly, a long one. No checklist will plan your lesson, mark your books or persuade your most challenging student that today is the day to start turning things around.

However, checklists can help you become a little more effective every day. They can help you put your time to better use, make your work more efficient and improve your communication with colleagues. They can reduce the number of points in the day when you are left sweating over something critical that you've completely forgotten. They can offer you some reassurance that, when going home at the end of the day, you've done everything that matters and can relax.

In the process, checklists can make you a better and a happier teacher.

I hope you find them useful. Let me know.

You can reach me via my blog improvingteaching.co.uk or on Twitter @hfletcherwood.

Bibliography

Bambrick-Santoyo, Paul (2012). *Leverage Leadership: A Practical Guide To Building Exceptional Schools* (San Francisco, CA: Jossey-Bass).

Catmull, Ed with Amy Wallace (2014). *Creativity, Inc. Overcoming the Unseen Forces That Stand In the Way of True Inspiration* (London: Bantam Press).

Covey, Stephen R. (2004). *The 7 Habits of Highly Effective People* (London: Simon & Schuster).

Danziger, Shai, Jonathan Levav and Liora Avnaim-Pesso (2011). Extraneous Factors in Judicial Decisions, *Proceedings of the National Academy of Sciences* 108(17): 6889–6892.

Day, Andy (2013). Piloting a Surgical Approach to Checklists, *Meridianvale* (24 November). Available at: https://meridianvale.wordpress. com/2013/11/24/piloting-a-surgical-approach-to-checklists/.

Didau, David (2015). *What If Everything You Knew About Education Was Wrong?* (Carmarthen: Crown House Publishing).

Fried, Jason (2010). Why Work Doesn't Happen At Work, *TED.com*. Available at: http://www.ted.com/talks/jason_fried_why_work_doesn_t_ happen_at_work?language=en.

Gawande, Atul (2010). *The Checklist Manifesto: How To Get Things Right* (London: Profile Books).

Heath, Chip and Dan Heath (2007). *Made to Stick: Why Some Ideas Take Hold and Others Come Unstuck* (London: Arrow).

Heath, Chip and Dan Heath (2010). *Switch: How To Change Things When Change Is Hard* (London: Random House).

Heath, Chip and Dan Heath (2013). *Decisive: How To Make Better Choices In Life and Work* (London: Crown Business).

Kahneman, Daniel (2012). *Thinking, Fast and Slow* (London: Penguin).

Lemov, Doug (2010). *Teach Like a Champion: 49 Techniques That Put Students On the Path To College* (San Francisco, CA: Jossey-Bass).

Lemov, Doug, Erica Woolway and Katie Yezzi (2012). *Practice Perfect: 42 Rules for Getting Better At Getting Better* (San Francisco, CA: Jossey-Bass).

Nuthall, Graham (2007). *The Hidden Lives of Learners* (Wellington: NZCER Press).

Pink, Daniel H. (2009). *Drive: The Surprising Truth About What Motivates Us* (New York: Canongate).

Phillips, Robert (2001). Making History Curious: Using Initial Stimulus Material (ISM) To Promote Enquiry, Thinking and Literacy, *Teaching History* 105 (December): 19–24.

Wiliam, Dylan (2007). Content Then Process: Teacher Learning Communities In the Service of Formative Assessment. In Douglas Reeves (ed.), *Ahead of the Curve: The Power of Assessment To Transform Teaching and Learning* (Bloomington, IN: Solution Tree Press), pp. 183–204.

Wiliam, Dylan (2011). *Embedded Formative Assessment* (Bloomington, IN: Solution Tree Press).

Willingham, Daniel T. (2009). *Why Don't Students Like School?* (San Francisco, CA: Jossey-Bass).

Many topics covered in the book are discussed at further length in my blog: http://improvingteaching.co.uk.